D1431003

WORD AND REVELATION

WORD
AND REVELATION

Essays in Theology I

HANS URS VON BALTHASAR

HERDER AND HERDER

1964
HERDER AND HERDER NEW YORK
232 Madison Avenue, New York 16, N.Y.

Translated from *Verbum Caro, Skizzen zur Theologie I,*
first part (Johannes Verlag Einsiedeln), by A. V. Littledale
with the cooperation of Alexander Dru.

Nihil obstat: Patrick A. Barry
　　　　　　Censor Librorum

Imprimatur: ✠ Robert F. Joyce
　　　　　　Bishop of Burlington
　　　　　　March 20, 1964

Library of Congress Catalog Card Number: 64–19725
© 1964 by Herder and Herder, Incorporated
Printed in the United States of America

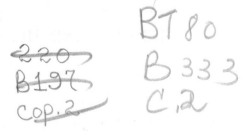

CONTENTS

Introduction

The papers collected in this volume are not formal theological treatises as such. Rather, as outlines and suggestions, they pattern the general nature of a sketchbook, and make no claim to finality. Human work however is necessarily incomplete, so that it may well happen that here and there we will, as it were, catch on the wing an idea that a more academic work may overlook. Nor should it be surprising that in a sketchbook certain themes constantly recur, that various concepts are approached and studied from many angles—this kind of repetitiveness and overlapping is due to the fascination generated by the unseen core of the subject matter. The figure studies of Rodin or Marées for example consist of outline sketches of an arm or a leg super- or juxtaposed; whether they represent a groping after the one correct curve, or whether, in fact, they represent the only possible way of reproducing human motion is impossible to ascertain. And so it is with the following essays in theology.

THE WORD, SCRIPTURE AND TRADITION

Scripture is the word of God that bears witness to God's word. The one word therefore makes its appearance as though dividing into a word that testifies and into a word to whom testimony is given. The word testified to is Jesus Christ, the eternal word of the father, the word who took flesh in order to witness, represent and be, in the flesh, the truth and life of God. The entire revelation concerning salvation is ordered to this manifestation of the word, as to a central point—in a forward direction in the apostles and in the whole history of the church to the end of time, in a backward direction in the old testament revelation in word and history, backward to the law and the prophets and even to the creation; for God upholds all things by the word of his power (Heb 1:3), creates all things through, for and by his word. The word is at the head of all things and by him all things consist (Col 1:16–17); and not only is the word the divine logos, for the son of man is the first and the last (Ap 1:18).

The testifying word is the sequence of scripture from Genesis to the Apocalypse which accompanies the progressive revelation of the word in the flesh and which reflects it as if a mirror—a function which distinguishes[1] it from the former word. The word of revelation is the word in the mode of action: God is apprehended in the act of self-communication. The word of scripture is the word in the mode of contemplating his own action, recording and elucidating it, something which can only be performed properly and perfectly by the word himself, since God alone compasses the entire range of his revelation; and only he can assign a valid human expression for it. The word of revelation is primarily the son, who speaks of the father through the Holy Spirit. The word of scripture is primarily the work of the Holy Spirit who as Spirit of the father effects, accompanies, illumines and clarifies the son's incarnation (before and after the event), and who as Spirit of the son, embodies his self-manifestation in permanent, timeless forms.

At first sight therefore the two lines of the testified and the testifying word seem to run parallel, but this appearance is deceptive. For both forms of the word are ultimately the one word of God testifying to itself in the one revelation.

Two sets of considerations can help clarify this concept.

1) There are, it is true, certain passages in which the contrast between the two forms of the word is plainly evident. In the gospel for example the lord speaks, acts and suffers without reference to the written account, i.e. to the

[1] In this distinction we part company with many protestants. Scripture is not identical with revelation. And although it is truly God's word it is so only in the mode of testifying to his revelation. Scripture is in fact only the mode of God's self-witness in words, while there are besides other modes of his self-witness.

10

gospel. This account was written down only later by eye-witnesses under the guidance of the Holy Spirit, who is already active here as the Spirit of the church. The Spirit has become, as it were, the most attentive hearer of the word, but who, because he himself is a divine person, sets down the divine truth in writing such as he heard it as Spirit and as he deems it important for the church. The same is true for all that the apostles did and for the book of the Acts, as well as for all the historical books of the old testament, although the two forms of the word are far less distinct in the prophets and in the Apocalypse. It is true of course that even then the word may first have come to the prophets personally, in a "private" revelation, and the publication made subsequently, in which case it makes no difference whether this revelation was first oral and afterward put in writing, or whether, on occasion, it was taken in written form from the outset. Revelation to the prophets and promulgation by the prophets tend to merge together, and form virtually a single act of revelation effected by the Spirit in the service of the coming or past incarnation of the son. Both acts constitute so complete a unity that there is no reason to postulate a revelation prior to its committal to writing, as for instance in the sapiential books where the revelation is transmitted directly to the pen of the inspired writer. The same is true for the epistles of the new testament. Admittedly, in the seven letters of the Apocalypse, a certain distinction is required inasmuch as the Spirit first dictates the letters to the churches to the apostle John who then, either at once or at some later time, writes them down; the same is not true of the other epistles. Yet

11

we must not overlook the expository, quasi-contemplative character of both the sapiential books and the apostolic epistles. Just as the former interpret the history of the Jews and their law for the people of God, so do the latter interpret the gospel for the church. The upshot is that the relationship between the testified and the testifying word is a fluid one, varying from clear contrast to actual identity. Revelation then is effected partly before the writing, partly in the actual writing; in other words scripture participates in God's self-revelation in Jesus Christ through the spirit.

2) The second line of thought takes us deeper, and definitely rules out the idea of a parallelism between the testified and the testifying word. The central word which God speaks and which comprises, as their unity and end, all the manifold words of God is Jesus Christ, the incarnate God. He however made his appearance in the sign of obedience, to fulfill the will of the father, and thereby to redeem and justify the creation. He fulfills it inasmuch as he lets his earthly life as word made flesh be fashioned, step by step, by all the forms of the word in the law and the prophets. His life is a fulfilling of scripture. Therefore he assimilates the scriptural word into his own life, making it live and there take flesh, become wholly actual and concrete. As his life proceeds two things stand out: the word more and more becomes flesh, inasmuch as he imparts to the abstract nature of the law and the expectancy of prophecy the character of a divine, factual presence, and the flesh becomes more and more word, inasmuch as he increasingly unifies the scriptural words in himself, making his earthly life the perfect expression of all the earlier revelations of God. He is their

12

living commentary, their authentic exposition, intended as such from the beginning. He fulfills not only the word of the father coming down from heaven, but equally the word stored up for him in history and the tradition of scripture —the word, that is to say, both in its vertical and horizontal provenance. If he, as the one finally come, is the complete, definitive fulfillment he is also, as a living person, the progressive, continual fulfillment. And since he is both of these in one, and always remains such, the possibility ensues of there being scripture even after him, though of a quite different character. The law and the prophets were like the formal presignifying of the word that would, at some time, become man: they were God's word in human form and, indeed, the adequate expression of revelation, a word not to be superseded or regarded as of merely relative significance. In this respect the word of the old testament served to define exactly the point of mediatorship, the place and the form in which God was to become accessible to man and of service to him. It was not without reason then that the law drawn up for the men of that time had as one of its functions the foreshadowing of the eucharist of the new testament; see for example Ps 118. And although Jesus made his life as man the compendium of all the scriptures, and realized in himself all its promises of eternal life (Jn 5:39–40), still there can be a scripture subsequent to him; and this fact is proof that the fulfillment of the father's decree does not imply its annihilation; that Jesus' fulfillment is not a conclusion (as in human affairs) but rather a new opening (as always with God); that he makes fulfillment issue in a new promise so as to remain at all times what he is, namely

13

the one who ever and again fulfills beyond all expectation.[1]
The lord remains in the flesh what he is, the word. He does
not dissociate himself from what had been said before his
coming, nor from what he himself has said or from what is
said about him. The gospel is the living doctrine proceeding
from him, become scripture, and abiding in the church, but
also a new "incarnate" scripture, a living participation in
his own corporeal nature (as the fathers repeatedly testify),
and therefore in his own quality of being inspired. Just as
the word he spoke as man is inspired by the Holy Spirit,
so also is the written word; its inspiration is not something
past and concluded but a permanent, vital quality adhering
in it at all times. It is this quality which allows the lord to
adduce the word as proof that, in his fulfillment in the
Spirit, he transcends all boundaries, all verbal limitations,
in his superabundance of life and power. If then the incarnate son merges all scripture in himself so as to make it
fully what it is, namely the word of God the father in the
son, he also sends it forth from himself so as to make it
fully what it is, namely the word of the Spirit whom he
sends out at the end of his earthly course, upon his return to the father. In both forms therefore scripture is not

[1] "My words shall not pass away: we may ask whether it is not the
case that the words of Moses and the prophets have passed away, and
those of Christ not passed away; for what they prophesied has passed
away by being fulfilled, but the words of Christ are ever full, ever in
process of fulfillment; they fulfill themselves every day, nor are
they ever overfilled. It is they, in fact, that are fulfilled in the saints,
that are being fulfilled, that will be fulfilled in the future. Or else perhaps we should say that the words of Moses and the prophets are
perfectly fulfilled, since, in their true sense, they are also words of the
son of God, and are always being fulfilled." Origen, *Comm in Mt*
Nr 54, Berlin edition, vol 2, 123–24.

14

a testifying word separated from the testified but rather the one word of God in the unity of his incarnation.

In this connection the patristic idea that scripture is the body of the logos receives added significance. If however we are not to view it as a merely arbitrary piece of allegorizing, we must place it more precisely in the whole setting of the incarnation.

The expression body of Christ can be used in many senses. The basic and primary meaning is the historical body which he took from Mary, in which he lived on earth, with which he ascended to heaven. The final form and purpose of his taking flesh is the mystical but nonetheless real body, the church, the incorporation of humanity into the historical body, and thereby into the Spirit of Christ and of God. And to make it plain that the historical and the mystical body are not two disparate things but are a unity in the strict sense, there exist two means to effect incorporation, two means which bring about the transition from the first to the second bodily form: the eucharist and scripture. They mediate the one, incarnate logos to the faithful, and make him who of himself is both origin and end the way (via); the eucharist does so inasmuch as he is the divine life (vita), and scripture inasmuch as he is the divine word and the divine truth (veritas). The eucharist is the marvelous means of freeing Christ's historical humanity from the confines of space and time, of multiplying mysteriously its presence without forfeiting its unity and, since it is given to each christian as his indispensable nourishment (Jn 6:53–58), of incorporating all into the body of Christ, making

15

them in Christ one body through which courses the divine life. Through the eucharist the church comes into being as the body of Christ; and while the one flesh of the lord is multiplied mankind divided is unified in it. "And the bread that we break, is it not the partaking of the body of the lord? Because the bread is one, we though many, are one body, all of us who partake of the one bread" (1 Cor 10:16–17).

Scripture contains the lord as word and as spirit, in the same marvelous transcendence of space and time, without the word ceasing to be unique and individual. Just as the eucharist does not mean that Christ's body ceases to be the one, historical body, so his word in scripture does not detract from its being present as a unique concrete reality. The two modes of communication have this in common: they universalize the body of Christ without making it any the less concrete. The universal validity of the words of scripture is not to be attributed to the abstract and universal nature of general truths of the human order. Scripture makes the incarnate lord present in a way analogous to that in which the eucharistic body makes present his historical body. Hence Origen admonishes Christians to approach the word in scripture with the same reverence as they approach the lord's body in the eucharist. The patristic tradition is continued in these words of the *Imitation of Christ:* "Two things are needful for me in this life, and without these two I cannot continue to live: God's word is light, and his sacrament living bread, for my soul. We can also say that they are two dishes set out in the room of God's church. One is the dish of the holy altar; on it lies the sacred bread, the precious body of Jesus Christ. The other

16

is the dish of the holy law; on it lies the sacred doctrine which instructs us into the true faith, and reaches, behind the veil, into the inmost holy of holies" (LV, 11). "The catholic church, next to the body and blood of the lord, deems nothing so sublime and holy as God's word in sacred scripture" (Origen). Both of them are made possible only through the historical Christ and his body the church; they are both exclusively the gift of the bridegroom to the bride, and for those outside they are always inaccessible and alien. It is recorded of the martyrs that they died rather than surrender the sacred scriptures to the heathens, just as Tarsicius died to prevent the eucharist from falling into their hands. Both forms are express results of the Spirit acting on what pertains to the son; to the Spirit is to be attributed equally the miracle of transubstantiation and the formation of the word in scripture. Indeed it is the work of the Spirit to form the mystical body of Christ by spiritually universalizing the historical Christ. The profound truth of their relationship is not affected by the fact that scripture does not contain the word in the manner of a sacrament. For the lord is at all times ready to give himself to and work in those who receive him in a lively spirit of faith; and he is no less ready to reveal himself in person, as word and truth, to those who approach the scripture praying, seeking and thirsting. "Per evangelica dicta deleantur nostra delicta."

All this brings out clearly the relationship between scripture and tradition. The word of scripture is a gift of the bridegroom to his bride the church. It is destined for the church and, in this respect, belongs to her; but it is also the

17

word of God, the word of the head, and as such it is above
the church. This variable relationship in which the church
exercises control over scripture, but only insofar as God's
word allows her to do so, is best clarified by the mysterious
relationship between bride and bridegroom, a mystery of the
divine love. For the more God, in human form and therefore
divested of power, delivers himself over to the church in
order to exalt and enrich her the more must the church
humble herself as his handmaid, and adore, in the son's
humiliation, his sublimest majesty. If then she recognizes
tradition as a source of the faith alongside scripture, it is
far from her intention to evade the authority of scripture
by appealing to traditions unknown, perhaps even formed
by herself. What she really means is that the letter of scripture can, after the incarnation, only be a function of his
living humanity which, in any case, transcends mere literal-
ness. Scripture itself witnesses to this: "Many other signs
also Jesus worked in the sight of his disciples, which are
not written in this book. . . . many other things that Jesus
did; but if every one of these should be written, not even
the world itself, I think, could hold the books that would
have to be written" (Jn 20:30; 21:25). Here the word that
testifies asserts that the word testified to, the word of revelation, is infinitely richer than what can be drawn from
scripture. And here the word after the incarnation is essentially different from the word before it. The old testament
word was only coming, not a word finally come and fulfilled. For that reason it could not have been the subject
of a "tradition" (meaning thereby the expression of the
fullness of the word manifested, a fullness that bursts all

18

the bounds of scripture.[1] Regarding the old testament word's expression of the law and the promises it was on a par with what could have been comprised in ordinary speech and writing—it being always understood that this also could only have been assimilated in faith and through the grace of God who spoke it. The Jews however had as an object of faith no other divine revelations to Abraham or Moses, no other divine word to the prophets, than that contained (whether from the outset or subsequently) in their scriptures. Consequently there was in the old covenant no tradition as a source of faith: the scriptural principle was similar to that of protestantism in relation to the new testament. For it is not so much the organic character of history, as the Tübingen theologians held, that makes tradition a source of faith from the time of the incarnation, but primarily the uniqueness of the person of Christ and of his relationship to his mystical body, the church. But for tradition the scriptures of the new covenant would resemble those of the old covenant, having its law and promises; it would not be the word-body of him who also dwells and works in his church as the living eucharistic body (not present in the old covenant).

In this the eschatological character of strict protestantism, which denies the mass and transubstantiation, is perfectly logical. The God of the old covenant speaks from heaven in

[1] There was of course tradition in the human sense, insofar as the fixing of the word in writing came later and harked back to the traditions of centuries—a normal procedure with ancient peoples. This kind of tradition is a sort of pregnancy whose purpose is the bringing forth of a child fully formed, namely the word of scripture. In the new testament however scripture is present at the beginning of the church's history, and thus immersed in tradition, which is its vehicle.

explicit language, but he does not deliver himself up to the people. But Christ delivers himself up to the church because he has delivered himself for her on the cross (Eph 5:2; 5:25), because the father delivered him up to the cross for her (Rom 8:32), because he finally delivered up his Spirit on the cross (Jn 19:30), the Spirit he breathed on the church at Easter (Jn 20:22). So it is that he delivers himself over to the church as eucharist and as scripture, places himself in her hands in these two corporeal forms in such wise that, in both forms, he creates a means of being present in the church as the one, ever active, unchanging life, life that is yet infinitely manifold, ever manifesting itself in new, astonishing ways. The word of revelation infinitely surpasses all that the word that testifies can possibly contain; and this superfluity becomes available to the church in the living eucharistic presence of Christ; the necessary reflection of this vitality in verbal form is the principle of tradition. Scripture is itself tradition inasmuch as it is a form whereby Christ gives himself to the church, and since there was tradition before scripture, and since there could have been no scriptural authority apart from tradition. At the same time scripture, as the divinely constituted mirror of God's revelation, becomes the warrant of all subsequent tradition; without it the church's transmission and proclamation of the truth would be imperiled, in fact made impossible—and the same is true for her holiness—without the presence of the eucharist.

The word of scripture, as God's word bearing witness to itself, is essentially threefold, being word of God, God's word concerning the world, God's utterance to man.

1) *Word of God.* It is word, not vision, not feeling, not

20

mere halting speech, such as human speech about God would be at best. A word, that is, of unequaled clarity, simplicity, precision. This character of the word derives from the two mysteries of the trinity and the incarnation. Since God has in himself the eternal word that expresses him eternally, he is most certainly expressible; and since this very word has taken human form and expresses in human acts and words what it is in God, it is capable of being understood by men. The first would be of no avail for us without the second, the second unthinkable without the first. The identity of Christ's person in his two natures as God and man is guarantee of the possibility and rightness of the reproduction of heavenly truth in earthly forms, and of its accuracy in Christ. "Amen, amen, I say to you, we speak of what we know, and we bear witness to what we have seen . . . He who comes from heaven is over all. And he bears witness to that which he has seen and heard" (Jn 3:11, 32). But this truth of God, with all its precision, is yet personal (the word being the person of the son), and therefore sovereign and free. The son is not some kind of mechanical reproduction of the father; he is that regiving which is effected only by perfect love in perfect sovereignty. For this reason the translation of the divine word into a human word is itself, through the son, sovereign and free, and not verifiable other than in the son himself. "I am the truth." "No man comes to the father but by me." Faith therefore, bringing acceptance of the word, is demanded in that the truth proclaimed is primarily divine (and so surpassing human understanding) and, secondly, personal, that is to say, brought about only by trusting in the freedom of the divine person who forms it; for in fact the exact correspondence between the divine content and the human expression is inseparable from the person of the incarnate word of God, being itself the effect of the incarnation. In other words the relation between the human and the divine in scripture finds its measure and norm in the relation between the divine and human natures in Christ. And just as the whole of Christ's humanity is a means of expressing (principium quo) his divine person (principium quod), and this in turn being the expression of the father, so each word of scripture is a purely human word, but yet, as such, wholly the expression of a divine content.

This concept illustrates how the much discussed relationship between the literal and spiritual senses of scripture is a christological problem, one soluble only on the basis that the two senses are to each other what the two natures of Christ are to each other. The human nature we come into contact with first; it is the medium covering yet revealing the divine element, becoming transparent in the resurrection, but never, in all eternity, to be discarded or disparaged. The spiritual sense is never to be sought "behind" the letter but within it, just as the father is not to be found behind the son but in and through him. And to stick to the literal sense while spurning the spiritual would be to view the son as man and nothing more. All that is human in Christ is a revelation of God and speaks to us of him. There is nothing whatever in his life, acts, passion and resurrection that is not an expression and manifestation of God in the language of a created being.

The perfect correspondence the son effects between expression and content does not imply that the content, which is divine and indeed God himself, does not surpass the ex-

22

pression, which is in created terms. Christ's divinity cannot be wholly comprehended through his humanity, and no more can the divine sense of scripture ever be fully plumbed through the letter. It can only be grasped in the setting of faith, that is to say, in a mode of hearing that never issues in final vision, but in a progression without end, a progression ultimately dependent, in its scope, on the Holy Spirit (Rom 12:3; Eph 4:7). Faith, the foundation of all our understanding of revelation, expands our created minds by making them participate in the mind of God, disclosing the inward divine meaning of the words through a kind of coworking with God (1 Cor 2:9, 16); for this reason it is the saint, the man most open to the working of the Spirit, who arrives at the closest understanding. He will not do what the ordinary man, so dominated by original sin, does almost unawares, yet with such desperate persistence: confine the meaning of God's word within human bounds, admitting its truth only to the extent that it corresponds to human forms of thought and ways of life, and content himself with the meaning he has managed to elicit at some time or other, as if it was the final one, attempting to do what the Magdalen was forbidden: "Touch me not (i.e. do not keep clinging to me), for I am not yet ascended to my father" (Jn 20:17). The idea that one has understood a passage of scripture finally and completely, has drawn out all that God meant in it, is equivalent to denying that it is the word of God and inspired by him. For the effect of inspiration is not to be seen principally in the absence of error in scripture, which is only a by-product of inspiration —many a book is free from error without thereby being inspired. Inspiration involves a permanent quality, in virtue

23

of which the Holy Spirit as auctor primarius is always behind the word, always ready to lead to deeper levels of divine truth those who seek to understand his word in the
Spirit of the church, the Spirit she possesses as bride of
Christ. The primary content of scripture is always God himself. Whether it is narrating historical events, enunciating
laws or relating parables, God is speaking and speaking
about himself, telling us what he is and about the manner
in which he surveys and judges the world. To penetrate into
the spirit of scripture means to come to know the inner
things of God and to make one's own God's way of seeing
the world.

2) Scripture then as the word of God is also his *word
concerning the world,* and this, once again, only in relation
to its union with the word of revelation, which is the incarnate son, precisely because God has made the son the
source of the meaning of the world and sees it in no other
connection than in the son. In him it was created: the "in
the beginning" of creation (Gn 1:1) is to be seen in relation to the "in the beginning was the word" (Jn 1:1). Consequently it was created for him as its end, just as, firstly,
"we" the believers (Eph 1:4) and then "all men" (1 Tim
2:2–6), indeed "all things in heaven and on earth," were
to be planned, chosen, created and reestablished (Eph
1:10) in him, so that he, as "first and last," holds the keys
of all (Ap 1:18). This he is not only as logos but as incarnate and crucified. "God did not plan the foundation of
the world and bring it to pass without, in foreseeing sin,
form his decree for the redemption of the world, and this
through the future incarnation of his only-begotten son.
Redemption therefore is not something in the mind of God

24

posterior to the creation of the world. On the contrary the world was created in the foreknowledge of its need for redemption, for it to be the stage on which redemption should be enacted. Consequently, it is not only through the eternal Word that this world was conceived from eternity and created by God, but, rather, for the sake of the Word, who was to take flesh, who became flesh and dwelt among us."[1]

Since then the whole creation is formed in, through and for the son it participates, in its very root, in his formal character as word. The son as the word incarnate is the supreme and dominant law of the world. This idea is like an eminence from which we may look back and see the word of God—that is, the law and the promise, the form of the word selected by God to enshrine his dealings with mankind—as an anticipation and as a kind of basic setting of the incarnation. And we may also go back beyond the old testament and say the same of that form of the word set in the heart of creation itself, in the "nature" of the creature, replacing for the gentiles, in whose hearts it was engraved, the law and promise given exclusively to the Jews (Rom 2:14–15). In both cases, that of the Jews and of the gentiles, the presence of the word of God within them was the center of gravity and ruling principle of their lives. A human being means one to whom God has spoken in the word, one who is so made as to be able to hear and respond to the word. The alexandrian theology, which derives the rational character of the creation (in a wider sense also the rationality of the subhuman creation) from the presence of the logos within it, agrees here with modern philosophers such as Dilthey, Heidegger, Kamlah, who see the signi-

[1] Loch und Reischl, *Die hl Schrift* 1885, re Eph 1:4–5.

25

ficance of the derivation of "Vernunft" (reason) from "Vernehmen" (perception), or Buber and Ebner, who place the essence of created being in its capacity for and capability of the word. Maximus the Confessor even declared that there are three stages in the realization of the word in the world: the word as nature, the word as scripture and the word made flesh in Christ. Accordingly the law of history and that of nature is, ultimately, to be measured by the law of Christ, the final and definitive logos of the entire creation, for man finds the word that expresses and "redeems" him only in hearing and vitally responding to the word of God in Christ. However secular this human word may seem as culture, art, philosophy, pedagogy and technology, it can yet be a response to God's call, and so a bringing back of man and the world to God. Thus in responding to God's word man will also be enabled to "redeem" the word lying deeply hidden in the nature of things, to say what each thing says (Claudel) and, himself infused through Christ by the word, to express the creation subjected to him. But this ordering exacts from man that, the more he approaches the summit, Christ, the more acute should become his perception of the word's concretization in history. In nature the word is present in a permanent state, in history it is present in individual events, in revelation it has that actuality and singularity of God which transcends all the laws of historical time, just as God reveals himself in the "one man Jesus Christ" (1 Tim 2:5) in an ever-present "today" (2 Cor 6:2; Heb 4:7) without any diminution or staleness.

3) Scripture therefore is *God speaking to man*. It means a word that is not past but present, because eternal, a word

26

spoken to me personally and not simply to others. Just as the
eucharist is not merely a memorial of a past event but makes
eternal and ever-present the single, living body and sacrifice of the lord, so scripture is not mere history but the form
and vehicle of God's word addressing us here and now.
Man's life, at its deepest level, is a dialogue with God but
one in which God's word to man is infinitely more important than man's to God, and man can respond as he
should only through a constant hearing of the word (contemplation must here be understood as listening). Furthermore all that God has to say to any man he has spoken
once and for all in Christ (Heb 1:1), so that each of us
must individually acknowledge and make his own all the
treasures of wisdom and knowledge hidden in Christ (Col
2:3). When, finally, we consider that scripture is the divine
testimony made by Christ, it is clear that reading and contemplating scripture in the spirit and guidance of the
church is the most certain means of discerning what, in
the concrete, is God's will for my individual life and destiny, of discovering the means appointed by him. It is here
that God has spoken, here that he never ceases to speak in
the fullness of his word. From this source the preacher steeps
himself in the knowledge of the things he has to impart to
his hearers, while here each individual believer encounters
God's word addressed to him personally in the most direct
fashion. Every word that proceeds from the mouth of God
is, as the lord has said, nourishment for the soul (Mt 4:4).
Thomas Aquinas comments: "One who does not nourish
himself on the word of God is no longer living. For, as the
human body cannot live without earthly food, so the soul
cannot live without the word of God. But the word proceeds

27

from the mouth of God when he reveals his will through the witness of scripture" (*Cat aurea* in Mt 4:4). The word of scripture is above any other word concerning God; in virtue of its christological form it is a word opening into God and leading into him. To phrase this in human terms, it is selected by the Holy Spirit with such art that its precision never involves limitation (as is the case with human utterance), that the single truth it conveys does not rule out any other truth, whether allied, contrasting or complementary; it never bolts any door but opens all locks. Even the church's definitions, though infallible and assisted by the Holy Spirit, do not share this special quality of scripture, for their significance is mostly to put an end to a period of uncertainty, to solve a point of doubt or controversy, rather than to engender a fresh perspective.[1] However necessary these definitive pronouncements may be for the church in history they are by no means the basic sustenance of the christian.

Since God's truth through Christ is imparted to the soul in scripture no dialogue between God and the soul, however interior or mystical, ever takes precedence of scripture or replaces it. This must be asserted to counter the protestant tendency to emphasize, on the one hand, the prophetic against the mystical element (Heiler), and on the other the word against mysticism (Brunner). To oppose the two is either to revert to an old testament idea of the word, ignoring its aspect as food of the soul and, therefore, its

[1] As Scheeben justly observes: "A diligent comparison and reflection on the expressions and indications of holy scripture affords . . . a fuller, deeper and more comprehensive understanding of revealed truth than is given in the authoritative dogmatic teaching of the Church" (*Dogmatik* 1, 122).

28

likeness to the eucharist, or else to misconceive the nature of christian mysticism, whose only possible norm is revelation as contained in scripture. Scripture itself is mystical not only in its being inspired, inspiration being of the mystical order, but also because the whole of it, the old testament as well as the new, describes the continuous sequence of mystical experiences undergone by the patriarchs, prophets, kings, apostles and disciples. It would be far better for christian mysticism to recognize in scripture its true canon, instead of diverting into the obscurities of individual psychology. Christian mysticism is scriptural mysticism, that is to say, a special charismatic form of encounter with the word. Its function, direct or indirect, is to convey the revelation of the word to the church; thus it is essentially social. The Spirit lives through the centuries in the church as the inspired author of the scriptures, and is ever at work in interpreting the revealed word, leading the church deeper "into all truth" (Jn 16:13); and it continues to act in the "prophets" of the new testament—those who, along with the apostles, Paul considered foundations of the church (Eph 2:10; 3:5; 4:11), in the same manner that he included the prophets of the old testament. Admittedly their writings are not sacred scripture in the biblical sense, but only because, with the lord and with his eyewitnesses, God's revelation had already reached its completion; and therefore scripture, as the form of the word testifying to this revelation, had likewise been completed.

However, where revelation is concerned, it is best to avoid speaking of a "conclusion." The word is inappropriate since the completion of fullness is not so much an end as a beginning. It is the beginning of the infinite pouring out of

29

Christ's fullness into that of the church, of the church's growth into the fullness of Christ and of God, as described in the epistle to the Ephesians. It is moreover the beginning of the outpouring of the infinite riches of scripture into the church, whose range the whole of world history will never suffice to exhaust. Every human book is finite in content. Each can be studied, read, committed to memory, until one day it is mastered and no longer needed. But scripture is the word of God; and the more we probe it the more do its divine dimensions broaden and impose themselves. "Strengthened with power through his Spirit . . . you may be able to comprehend with all the saints what is the breadth and length and height and depth"—the four-dimensional space of divine truth!—"and to know Christ's love which surpasses all knowledge, in order that you may be filled unto all the fullness of God" (Eph 3:18–19).

THE WORD AND HISTORY

1

Word here means the word of God in Jesus Christ. And by history we do not mean exclusively what the christian might describe as the imperceptible process of mankind's advance to salvation, namely the actions of the individual and of the whole community as governed by the just judgment and grace of the word that is Christ. Nor do we mean solely secular history as depicted in textbooks and treatises. Rather we take the word to indicate the entire involved complex of temporal events that can never be wholly of a public nature, since their deepest currents belong to the personal domain, or purely secular, since their strongest driving forces derive from a philosophical or religious commitment, from a man's belief or unbelief, love or hate, hope in one direction or another or refusal of hope. A purely secular view of history is quite impossible. Historical science may attempt to be neutral as regards the philosophy of history but it cannot controvert the fact that its subject—man in his acts and sufferings—conducts himself, in small things and in great, according to his basic idea of ultimate meaning, that is to say, as a philosopher.

Thus the science of history passes naturally into the philosophy of history—always immanent within it—since no one can describe without partisanship the efforts of mankind in general to discover the meaning of life and action in time. To solve this question history can only resort to action, whose inner dialectic however, as it proceeds, cancels the meaning previously accepted and allows a fresh one to emerge; events are judged by events on an inner-worldly level so that, in this sense, world history is judgment of the world from within it. But this hard and implacable judgment of the hegelian "directing world spirit," a spirit we have lately seen and experienced once again and which brings a salutary disillusionment to human imaginings, is far from being the kind of judgment that satisfies the deepest and most just aspirations of the human spirit. And its failure is more pronounced in proportion as man's goal becomes more rational through self-consciousness and self-direction. Neither the prechristian nor the christian conception of history claimed to solve the problem of the inner meaning and movement of history through a consideration of the course of events. The only "solution" achieved in this manner was through a reduction of the real metaphysical questions to a superficial, arid pattern of historical "progress." This pattern in turn can be made to serve as the key to the whole only by misconceiving, indeed depreciating the meaning and value of the human person and the whole philosophy of man. A philosophy of history which does not take account of the "mystery" of meaning but which offers a final solution, a clear explanation of the beginning and end of history, is ridiculous from the outset, just as any philosophy is that claims to be able to define being and ex-

32

istence. The perpetual contrast between individual and social eschatology is a potent warning for all philosophies of history against toying, even in thought, with final "solutions." The meaning of the individual and his life of toil is not to be sacrificed either to the hegelian world spirit or to the marxist collectivity or to the american idea of progress; yet, at the same time, neither can the meaning of history be reduced simply to the question of the individual. The problem of existence presupposes not only psychologically but ontologically that the solution is possible. The very helplessness of temporal existence is the ground for the consoling postulate of eternity, even though the consolation may at times elude us; it even appears in Nietzsche's absurd philosophy of eternal recurrence: the human freedom to question, in positing itself, desires to transcend itself by affirming and assenting to the being given in the act of existing.

For the believing christian however God's salvific action, his redemption of the sinful world through Christ, is present within human history. There is, within the time that passes away, a "fullness of time" in Christ, born under Augustus and dying under Pilate and Tiberius, in the epiphany of God to whom Asia paid homage in the person of the three kings, and at whose death, according to Dionysius, the heavens were darkened even in egyptian Heliopolis (*ep* 7); there is moreover a resurrection of the buried Christ, testified to by a definite number who saw him (1 Cor 15). Yet this salvific action passed almost unnoticed by world history, and the tremendous impact it subsequently unleashed on the course of history was in fact due to believers who, in the perspective of history, are not specially

33

distinguished from other believers and witnesses. The proofs
they adduced for the truth of their faith, namely the miracles
worked by its founder and his fulfillment of the old testament prophecies, necessarily presuppose the faith they support if their full force is to be perceived. Paul himself was
aware of this fact and used it as one of his principal argu-
ments for justifying his own life as an apostle, showing at
length and forcibly that it was only explicable on the basis
of the truth of his mission. And the longer the church continues the more conclusively does this witness pass from
individuals with apostolic and charismatic endowments
over to the church as a whole, which "in itself, by reason
of its marvelous expansion, sublime holiness and inexhaustible fecundity in all goods, its catholic unity and un-
conquerable persistence, is a great and ever-present motive
of credibility, and an irrefutable witness to its divine mission" (*Denz* 1794).

The very same church however is so firmly entrenched in
world history as to become part and parcel of it: after a
period of defiant indifference, on the ground of her supernatural qualities, to all that pertains to world history the
church has become so thoroughly versed in the methods of
mundane life and action—even to the point of assuming
all the usual secular modes of organization, even applying
force in discipline and punishment, and at times even applying force to secure conversions—that its administrative
structure was highly commended in an american survey of
large scale enterprises. The result is that the supernatural
mystery of its existence in history can no longer be supposed clearly evident to nonbelievers. On the contrary, from
the secular point of view, the historical influence of the

34

church is sufficiently explained by its initial powerful influence and by its subsequent skillful exploitation of the existing political situation. In our day the church is increasingly being forced to take the defensive, and it may well be that the future, though hardly the present, will bear eloquent testimony to unbelievers in support of the transcendental source of its historical greatness. In the earlier period of christendom when the secular and the spiritual elements were much more closely intertwined the organic quality (the living unity pervading all the members) was a visibly striking testimony to the presence of the Spirit. But now it is cast into the shade by the various forms of unity achieved in the secular sphere, and even surpassed by these purely human achievements; so that in the eyes of unbelievers it now works more to the disadvantage of christianity than for it. The church, now so deeply involved in the world, is assessed by it on secular standards, and found wanting. Had it the right to be so incarnate in history when it could promise the world no other form of salvation than one transcendent and eschatological? The reality it proclaims is essentially a hidden one which, as its founder himself foretold, would scandalize men and rouse opposition even to death. And the more mankind strives to organize itself—such action having necessarily an eschatological aspect, and so in competition with the transcendental christian eschatology—the more do faith and history seem hopelessly irreconcilable. Protestant views of history (e.g. those of Niebuhr, Löwith, Barth) developed from the supposition of such a cleavage.

In the present state of history there stands out, as never before since the founding of christianity, the power of the

word that Christ spoke and that he is. That the obscure
Galilean should have been the fullness of time cannot be
established by empirical means. But that he spoke words
which have since become part of and dominate world history, words without parallel either before or since, even
though obviously correlated with those of the prophets, is
no hidden fact but patently historical. They constitute the
link between the hidden workings of salvation, whose existence and significance they affirm, and world history, in
which they make themselves irresistibly heard. "Go therefore, teach all nations . . . all things whatsoever I have com-
manded you." Two things here demand a detailed explanation. The first is that since the word of Christ suddenly
emerges from a state of concealment this state alone is
what makes it comprehensible, and alone accounts for its
emergence; it emerges, that is, from a profound yet completely human consciousness of the mysteries of the trinity
and the redemption, from an overwhelming consciousness
of mission embracing the entire creation and, for this very
reason, a consciousness of the sacrifice to be accomplished,
of the surrender of his entire being to the world, the giving
of his flesh and blood, of the sacraments. It is this hidden
mode of existence that justifies the provocative and chal-
lenging nature of the word spoken, just as a gold deposit
justifies issuance of notes of high value; and the word itself
constantly recalls this prior existence, as in the provocative
statement "I am" and in the challenge to his enemies to
investigate every side of his life: "Which of you shall convince me of sin?"

This existence therefore can be examined and vindicated,

but its inner logic is only disclosed when interpreted from the standpoint of the word, that is, in relation to the trinity and the redemption. Consequently Christ's spoken word is the expression of this existence, its supreme authority needing no other justification than his own being—this was also the case with the prophets; but at the same time Christ's existence is wholly the word, since all that it comprises of action and decision is handed over to man's investigation and use. Thereby the human element in Christ is so prodigiously enriched that we are forced to apprehend the presence of God in this man, the presence of the mystery of the love and of the missions of the trinity at the heart of eternal life. This truth alone explains how the man Christ, in every particular, in his speaking and silence, his action and suffering, his prayer or mere presence, can be the perfect word, utterance, expression and image charged with spiritual power, the pure revelation of life; for if he were simply man human speech, in presuming to express God, would perforce lapse into incoherence and finally silence, as do all human theologies and mysticisms, whose highest form is apophatic. Christ's word on the contrary, though it conveys the hidden mystery of God better than any other word, does not collapse but correlates perfectly the object and the expression. It is not merely an approximation, not merely a groping after the right word, as if the same truth could be uttered in another way. All the events of a human life —birth, persecution, obscurity, prayer, temptation, decision, training of disciples, dealings with friends and enemies, conflict, resistance, flight, joy, sorrow, passion, death, burial —all that goes into the making of the life of Christ is so

37

pregnant and uncompromising in its significance, so comprehensible yet rich in meaning, that the word and its necessity are taken together, that the perfect correlation which makes all the human elements expressive of what is eternal points directly to the hypostatic union of God and man. Verba mea non transibunt. In this one instance the transposition of the divine, the wholly other, into the human attains absolute perfection. It succeeds not through human genius, reaching as it does with its creative imagination for the right image and expression, whether unconsciously or superconsciously, but through a simple act of obedience, permitting the Holy Spirit of the father so to act on the son's freedom as man that each of his individual decisions, each situation and encounter is in the end always infallibly and superlatively right. The son's obedience makes his whole life and being a continuous utterance of God to men. His obedience unto death is a state of abasement and self-annihilation, but it is precisely his "not my will" that allows the father to express himself totally in the son. And the Spirit who infuses this obedience in the son is, though the Spirit of the father, equally the Spirit of the son: qui a patre filioque procedit. Only thus is the fullness of time brought about.

In the old testament too God sent out his word to work mighty things (Ps 107:20; 147:15; Is 15:11); there were too in the old testament men who dedicated their entire lives in the service of the word; but the Spirit of God could never be the Spirit of the men obeying him. For this reason a man's obedience could never have been his perfect freedom. In that God's word created the covenant with his people the latter was without much reflection made the "expression" of God's revelation and a "word" for all people. Nonetheless this word, which objectively applied to all peoples and proclaimed the universality of redemption, was for the time being in the state of "promise," since the Israelite was a "hearer," one turned to God to receive the word he spoke, but one not a "bearer" of the word—which as a believer he could and should have brought to the pagan world. Only in Christ does man (which Christ is) become the word; but since this word is established and spoken it must also go out to all men; in him its mission is released and in him God's revelation becomes the word, which is identical with a man's individual existence. Therefore, in this man, man in general is addressed. The Jews did not cause the histories of Egypt and Babylon, still less that of Rome, even though God as lord of all "powers" made use of them to guide, punish and raise up Israel, even though the will of God concerning his people was made known to Pharaoh through Moses. But in the new testament the word of God is given as a man to man as such, and so to all peoples, given no longer in the vesture of a particular nation but in the nakedness of one human being to another. Thus the new covenant is far more profoundly "historical" than the old, despite all appearances to the contrary. And the community in conjunction with which the incarnate word places himself within history, that is, the Church, is not like Israel a kind of nation whose domestic events other people can disregard. It is on the contrary itself the expression, itself the vesture and message of the power of the incarnate God speaking to and governing the course of world history.

39

2

Now therefore we find ourselves situated, so to speak, on the other side of the word, which now looks not at what is behind—the existence of Christ as the son of God giving up his life freely in obedience for the life of the word—but at what is before—the world and its history. With this the word is directly confronted, and for this it has come into the world to determine its course. But, once we begin to consider this encounter, a doubt arises: surely then the word must be something so tremendous and radical that it can only be expressed in an eschatological setting, as John for instance describes it in the Apocalypse. In fact the word confronts history as its judge and savior, and the resultant situation is one where the momentousness of history is plainly apparent, where all previous misconceptions have been eliminated, and where no possible alternative between total belief and adoration and total rejection of the scandal of the cross is possible. The gospels all lead up to the point when the disciples, after their first flush of enthusiasm for the master, were, in all that happened later, culminating in the cross, the resurrection and ascension, raised above all human anticipations to the point of seeing in their companion and leader the lord of heaven and earth, and of announcing him as such to all peoples. So long as one has not reached this point or, having reached it, does not let it rule all his thinking, the essence of Christianity is wanting. For this reason any consideration of the relation between the word and history must start from eschatological reality and, having firmly established this, go back

40

to ask how this absolute principle that the word is the lord of all history can be applied within history so as to mean not only that he holds history in his grasp as judge and redeemer, but also, precisely as history, as a series of events in the human and mundane sphere, he forms and moulds it in detail. While protestant theology of history is content to limit itself to the first aspect, we hope to show that it necessarily includes and gives prominence to the second.

The incarnate word confronts history as its judge for the simple reason that he is the measure by which man is assessed. This he would be even if the word had never been spoken, had never been invested expressly with the office of judge. The mere existence of the just man assigns the sinner to his rightful place. Even the silent presence of the true standard is eloquent, for thereby the truth is firmly fixed. This aspect of Christ has something so absolute about it as almost to eliminate, by contrast, his subjective aspect, his design of redemption: "I have come a light into the world . . . if anyone hears my words, and does not keep them, it is not I who judge him; for I have not come to judge the world, but to save the world . . . The word that I have spoken will condemn him on the last day" (Jn 12:46f). Inasmuch as the word has been spoken once and for all through the son's life on earth, judgment has already been passed in principle: "The hour is coming, and now is here, when the dead shall hear the voice of the son of God" (Jn 5:25); the enemy is, in principle, overcome and the son can "wait" (Heb 10:15) for the word to have its final effect.

The pronouncements of the word create the obligation

41

to act accordingly, but this applies only to those who have to undergo judgment; as for the lord who judges, he always retains complete freedom and sovereignty. It is not as if the son's life and work were a kind of lifeless and rigid standard by which men are judged by God—otherwise they must fail completely, not only because they always fall short of what the son was and did but also because they are at enmity with him and have crucified him. But inasmuch as the son does the father's will, which is the salvation of sinners, he assumes, as redeemer, the father's office of judge, and since he has satisfied all the claims of justice he receives the freedom to make his own good pleasure the norm of judgment. A basic element in the justification of the sinner is a judgment and assessment, a free decision to see him in a particular light and no other, a supreme mystery and marvel of creative love which, desirous to see the sinner as a child of God, can actually bring about this status in his inmost being. Grace is essentially a mystery of the divine freedom, and it is precisely because of this fact that, here on earth, no philosophy of history is possible since the creative freedom of the judgment on men and events will only be revealed on the last day. From a purely human and historical standpoint life and the course of events are always incomplete in their being and significance. They are inherently ambiguous, capable of one or some other interpretation, and wait on a decisive word from the creator and redeemer to attain a being and significance valid in the face of, and for, eternity. Already in the world of time the word comes to men as a "two-edged sword" and thereby proves itself to be living and effectual (Heb 4:12); but this means that, even in time, there has begun

42

the separation between right and left (Mt 25:32), and it also shows that the relationship of man to the word remains a dialectical one right up to the last day. Christ not only foretold the fact of his coming judgment but also its content and procedure; and part of this content is that, despite the prophecy, both the good and the bad will be astounded by it: "When did we see you hungry?" (Mt 25:37,44). The freedom of the word is such that even when revealed and uttered it retains its full sovereignty and dominance over men. Even in the passion, and here especially for it is judgment actually passed in time, the law of the ecce praedixi vobis is verified: Peter's denial, which the word did not make necessary and inevitable, as well as the scandalizing of all the disciples, not to mention the crucifixion and resurrection—everything that happened had the character of something overpowering, something wholly unexpected. Everyone should have known that the son would rise again, but none of them believed it—and they were not naturally incredulous; only after the event did they find faith.

The freedom of the judgment on history comes out very clearly when it is viewed as an anticipation of the final judgment, itself correlative to the eschatological nature of the church—"The time has come for the judgment to begin with the household of God" (1 Pt 4:17), an echo of an old testament idea (Jer 25:29)—and the seven letters to the churches in the Apocalypse give as it were a specimen of the judgment in its relentless clarity both in approving and condemning. There we see how judgment on one and the same community runs the whole gamut from severity in reprobation to tenderness in election (letter to

43

Laodicea, 3:14f), and the subject judged has to admit at once the "rightness" of both extremes even though completely unable to perceive it beforehand. Should he find himself placed on the left side he must confess that he has deserved it. If through grace he is on the right hand he must likewise confess that the judgment of grace is just by reason of the work of Christ. Until this word of free assessment goes forth as the final utterance no assessment of history is possible. For its value is fluctuating all the while. Sin is so great that history could be entirely an object of reprobation. God "endures" it in "long suffering," in "patience," in mitigating his wrath, in "mildness," in "grace" (the theme of the sapiential books, repeated by Peter and James, a theme both semitic and hellenistic); but this "attitude" of God can never be presupposed and reckoned with by a philosophy of history aiming at objectivity. And at the same time the free judgment of God, or more precisely of Christ, is absolutely just, so patently just that "every mouth is stopped" (Rom 3:19), and no objection can be made even in thought. Because the one who judges is not the absolute God, who would seem to have no experimental knowledge of conditions governing the life of a created being (Job), but the man Jesus Christ who has himself experienced to the full the father's justice on the cross and at the resurrection. As a member of humanity he is contiguous with it; what is more he carries it in himself through his incarnation, the eucharist and the passion. He knows by experience its conditions of life, its temptations. He knows each one of its sins, having suffered them on the cross. He knows from within the stirrings of each individual who is, whether actually or only potentially, a member of

44

his mystical body. The judgment he freely makes is mankind's act of self-knowledge. But the truth about man can only be rendered visible in the procedure of rejecting some and choosing others (Mt 25), both free decisions. And this proves in the final analysis to be an act unifying what is seemingly disparate, rather than one dividing up mankind eternally, for on the cross the one "rejected," who bore all the world's guilt, is the "elect" par excellence.

Since judgment is already beginning in the house of God, and since the history of the church in the sight of the world is a portion of the revelation of the future judgment, the church judged takes its place at the side of the judge; being already "measured" it can, along with him, become the "measure" of the world. Christians judge the world and even the powers that rule the world ("angels," see 1 Cor 6:2–3). The reason ascribed down the ages, from the early fathers and Bede (in a lesson of the breviary) to Thomas Aquinas, is logical enough, namely that it is "specialiter" appropriate for those who "have left all things for Christ" to share the office of judging. Having the end of time always in view they have, from the outset, subjected the things of the earth to the measure and judgment of Christ.

3

Taking our stand then on eschatology we can now proceed to examine the relationship between the word and history in the historical setting. The limits within which this is possible are clearly shown by what has just been said. Yet

45

they are not so narrow as many catholics define them under the influence of protestant theology. For there is one dimension of the encounter between the word and history that is open to experience, and that in two respects. First of all there is the description of what the presence of the word of God has effected in world history, and continues to effect, together with the interpretation our minds bring to these facts. Secondly we may go further and tentatively seek, as the fathers did, to draw from the universal claims of the incarnate word certain clues to the whole economy disclosed by his involvement in the history of mankind.

1) As to the first we have already spoken of it by way of introduction. The presence of the word of God gives polarity to history. With the passing of the centuries it becomes ever more apparent that the word has overthrown all rival religions. It is verbum exterminans in a spiritual sense. The various rival religions are reduced to mere expressions of human religiosity, a process hastened by the impetus of the enlightenment and communism—a religiosity, that is, not in the meaning of Marx or Feuerbach but somewhat in that of Otto and Frazer; the revelation of the numinous is given along with the very nature of man. The rival religions are interchangeable as regards their essential core; this was already indicated at the end of the last century in Ramakrishna's experiment, which was conducted in terms of the different basic religions one after the other, and claimed to have the same religious experience in buddhist, islamic and, apparently, christian terms. It is only through man's reverting to the ideas, once discarded, of nationalism and racism that religions in the old sense have

revived. The future belongs to the "religious man" who will "tolerate" the different outward forms religion may take.

In contrast there is, solitary, and ever more solitary, the word of God as proclaimed by the church. The light however shines in the darkness, the world grows accustomed to its presence and, consciously or unconsciously, it borrows from christian teaching much that is desirable for mankind in the ethical, cultural and religious spheres. The proclamation of human rights is doubtless due to religious inspiration. The church is continually robbed and pilfered by secular humanism, whose aim is to take from her all that is useful to man, and to leave her only what is unserviceable, namely her absolute claims. "Et plagis impositis abierunt semivivo relicto." Nonetheless the church, which never ceases to be the light of the world, continues to present the word anew and in a living, vital way. The word is a challenge to each individual, and sooner or later he must accept or reject it. If he evades the encounter his evasion produces in him a deformation which is of his own making, his responsibility. There can no longer be any such thing as simple, untutored paganism; the word is so constituted that "no one can accuse it of sin." No one seriously impugns Christ's teaching—thus the church is maligned. She ought to appear visibly "redeemed," so that christians give scandal when they do not act according to the word they hear. Yet it is precisely the christian who is the first to place himself under the judgment of the word; thus the argument from scandal is inconclusive. The only sound objection against Christ was formulated by Ivan Karamasov in the account of the grand inquisitor, but in fact Dostoevsky turned his argument into a defense of the word's silence. Christianity,

47

said the inquisitor to the lord, is too hard for human nature; one who really knows man has to make concessions, lower the required standard. But this objection redounds to the honor of the word. It constitutes a fresh challenge to man on the part of the word, held fast in the prisons of the inquisition; for mankind will never bring itself to acknowledge in its midst the existence of a way of life that only one of them has carried through fully, even though innumerable others have followed his example, and to whom it ought to surrender unreservedly. Whenever anyone sets himself to pursue the highest ideal for mankind he must present himself to the word for the spiritual duel. The word issues its challenge to every person who wishes to make his mark on history; each person is summoned to confront it, and to have his achievement measured by the achievement of the word. The word is the goad of human civilization. The present confusion brought about by modern progress is in large measure a sign of flight from an encounter with the word.

2) But is not the word then some kind of incongruous element within world history, forming no part of it? Or is it possible to see a convergence of the two, a common history? On these questions opinions differ. The present trend is one of skepticism in reaction against any sort of hegelianism, one that rejects any attempt at a theological view of history that would be more than hypothetical. "New testament theology, as an eschatological exposition of the kingdom of God, is essentially indifferent to the political history of this world . . . Redemption as it works itself out does on occasion throw light on world history, but secular events are, as such, blind. Seen from the standpoint of the

new testament what determines the significance of Tiberius and Augustus, Herod and Pilate, is not their offices and actions but their role in God's plan of salvation. Jesus himself was born and crucified within an historical context, as a roman subject, but he had no intention of christianizing Rome and its empire."[1] But is this absolutely correct? "The fact," says Löwith,[2] "that Christ was born under the Rome of Augustus does not rule out, for the believing mind, that God could, had he so willed, have revealed himself in a previous epoch or two thousand years later, in Europe under Napoleon or in Russia under Stalin or in Germany under Hitler. Further, since the process of redemption, from beginning to end, concerns not kingdoms, nations or peoples but the individual soul there is no reason to deny that christianity might be quite unconcerned with the alternations of history, and even with the difference between civilization and barbarism. Both of these in fact reveal, under different conditions, one and the same nature of man, who was no less man at the beginning of history than he will be at the end."

Against this argument it could be objected that the transcendence of christianity as regards history should not be understood in the sense that Christ is not, at the same time, a real element within it, and therefore determined, as man, by his actual place in time and space. God's freedom must not be interpreted in a nominalist sense; the appeal to the potentia Dei absoluta, as opposed to the potentia ordinata, is, now as always, bad theology. And in the theol-

[1] Karl Löwith, *Weltgeschichte und Heilsgeschehen,* Die theologischen Voraussetzungen der Geschichtsphilosophie, Stuttgart 1953, 172f.
[2] Ibid 167.

ogy of history, as in all theology, the meaning (logos) is to be sought in the facts and not in what God could have done had he willed. If it is true that Christ is "the fullness of the Godhead corporeally" and that he brings this fullness into time, it is equally true that the relationship of time to Christ, both prior and subsequent to his coming, is far from being theologically irrelevant. Israel's history, precisely in its temporal sequence, always retains its significance as the way leading to the "fullness of time"—the stages are not to be inverted, abbreviated, eliminated. Relevant too is the history, obscure as it is when compared with Israel's, of the "gentiles" to whom yahweh, from the very beginning and increasingly as time went on, made known his demands and his dominion, and to whom on occasion he showed, as in a sudden flash, his providential designs for them in the salvation of the world. "For the sake of my servant Jacob and Israel my elect, I have even called you by your name. I have made a likeness of you, and you have not known me. . . . I girded you, and you did not know me" said yahweh to Cyrus (Is 45:4–5), the "messiah" (Is 45:1), the "friend" (48:14), the "predestined" (46:11). There is a course of action followed by various peoples and rulers that, unconsciously yet basically, obeyed God's ruling and so was in the line of the redemptive process. At the same time it is not identical with the divinely directed political course of great powers like Babylon and Egypt, through which God led Israel onward to its destiny, so long as it was obedient to him. Nor is it identical with the course pursued by Pharaoh in his persistent rejection of the revelation made to Moses and Aaron, and therefore clashing with the

50

redemptive process of history. But all this is only a prelude to the real drama since in the old testament the history of the chosen people is a national history.

The "fullness of time" is, historically speaking, characterized by the removal of the national boundary and by the extension of the redemptive process indiscriminately to all peoples. The elimination of the partition between Jews and gentiles is, as Paul demonstrates, grounded on the very essence of the mystery of redemption on the cross (Eph 2:11f) and brings about a highly dramatic situation through the encounter of two universalist conceptions, as developed by the historical theology of the epistle to the Romans, 9–11. The sphere beyond the "holy people" is, in principle, now brought in and illumined by the light of Christ and his word—"et quidem in omnem terram exivit sonus eorum." Theologically speaking the old testament distinction between sacred and profane history is no longer an essential one; it continues to be valid only so long as the particular form of the church remains necessary for her to proclaim and exemplify in her life the *universal* salvation already wrought. For it was to this church that, for forty days, the risen Christ opened the "sense for the understanding of the scriptures" and imparted his revealed theology of history— how she was to "preach and testify to all nations, beginning at Jerusalem" (Lk 24:44f). And all that, in the "last times," goes to the "development" of man, of his potentialities and endowments, and all that has profound repercussions on human history, is taken up into what is clearly the significance of the whole: development from fullness into fullness.

51

Here once again, and more peremptorily, arises the question of the secular significance of the redemptive "fullness of time." As to the history of the Jews it can be readily understood why its different stages had to come about for Christ to be manifested. They were stages of the "education of the human race" which (for we can now see better than Lessing could in his day) were not only stages of jewish history but also of mankind's self-consciousness, serving as an essential prerequisite of these jewish stages. For apart from a definite degree of consciousness of cultural and therefore religious unity in the area between Egypt and Babylon, the progression, in the time of Moses, from poly- and henotheism to strict monotheism is inconceivable; likewise the idea of the davidian kingship apart from the idea of the royal sonship of God. Nor are certain elements of classical and late jewish piety conceivable apart from the renewed contact with Babylon and, possibly, Iran; nor the spiritualized and ethical concepts of the sapiential books apart from contact with hellenism, the books wherein judaism became impregnated and liberated by the element that later, in Paul and John, was to make possible the complete universalization of the christian message. In fact, in the greek "miracle," as Heidegger brings out so forcibly, was accomplished the human mind's breakthrough from myth to philosophy, from magic to contemplation, from nationalism to fully achieved (for there were preliminary stages) internationalism and cosmopolitanism. In christianity the universalism of Christ encountered the greek conception of a nature common to all men, and this contact formed a spiritual basis for the christian mission. It was this widening of human consciousness which the "fullness of

52

time" awaited as its external prerequisite; consequently Jaspers' "axis time," though conceived in an antichristian sense, is absolutely, and in the traditional sense, a "praeparatio evangelica." Greek universalism was the human prerequisite for an understanding of the claims over mankind involved in Christ's works and teachings, just as over the centuries it has been the vehicle for those claims. The church took its origin in the coalescence of judeo-christianity and gentile christianity, and the pauline theology brings out clearly how the gentiles, though unable to add to Israel's "traditions of the fathers," still were by no means unable to contribute to the early stages of the church, if only in the assertion of its freedom from the old law.

The same coalescence which was at the basis of the theological fact of the church was also the foundation of the christian culture, understood not as a closed system alongside other cultures but as the culture resting on the word of God and its workings within history, and so the center to which every culture is polarized, whether positively or negatively, as we have shown. From the greek standpoint the imperium romanum was not simply one of the world kingdoms succeeding many others, but the first political embodiment of the idea of world unity that originated in Greece. This idea, despite its being frequently assailed and obscured, persists through all the centuries since Christ; the epoch of colonization, with its sudden vision of "one world," is no more than this encounter brought to fruition at the opportune moment, the kairos.[1] And the same kairos,

[1] Consider Claudel's *The Satin Slipper* in which this epoch is viewed as a symbol connecting the greco-roman period and our own; or Péguy's

in a deeper sense and now ineluctable, is our present time, in which after all the various national rivalries are played out, the question of the destiny of the world as a whole, presented to Caesar and Augustus, must now be faced. We can now see that this kairos, in which Christ has come, the encounter of these two universalisms, is, theologically, the final one, never to be superseded. However its immanent elements, its component parts, may develop, it will always be forced into the same point of contact with Christ, the transcendent element. Each new stage of consciousness means a new responsibility to hear the absolute word.

Once we recognize the theological significance of the intersection of the two universalisms the various stages of history backward from the time of Christ are seen each to have its own theological relevance. This means that the historical theology of the fathers, however mistaken in detail (such as the alleged dependence of Plato on Moses), was correct in its basic thesis: that alongside the jewish revelation history in its clearly visible course there proceeded a gentile salvation history whose course was obscure, and this we can only discern, apart from an occasional vivid glimpse, as in the case of Cyrus or the gentile "saints" of the old testament from Melchisedech and Balaam to Job, in its reflection in the jewish consciousness. The difference is vividly apparent. One, despite all the sublime aspects of its culture and religion, was ultimately mythology and idolatry—we have only to recall the horrible "religious" literature of the Phoenicians and Philistines which so strongly

---

Eve and the role he gives Athens and Rome, or his *Note Conjointe* and *Clio* with the interior encounter of Alexander and Christ, Felix and Polyeuctes.

54

influenced the psalms in their form. In the other we see the miracle of an experience of God given from above, purified and relentlessly driven forward at such a pace that, starting from nowhere, it led, within a few centuries, to the actual presence of Jesus Christ. Yet whatever took place in the shadow of sacred history, always providing the conditions for a fresh stage in the jewish consciousness, cannot, precisely for this help it gave, be "indifferent" as regards the history of redemption. Whatever God used as an instrument for his son's coming was taken up by him in the great recapitulation brought to pass in him. Admittedly however the gentiles remained up to his time in the "shadow of death" and, as far as salvation goes, without history. But from him a light shines out on their whole history, directly back to its origins, just as from Christ the light of justification shines back as far as Abraham, Noah and Adam. "Behold, I will establish my covenant with you, and with your seed after you. And with every living soul that is with you, as well in all birds, as in cattle and beasts of the earth, that are come forth out of the ark. . . . And the bow shall be in the clouds, and I shall see it, and shall remember the everlasting covenant that was made between God and every living soul of all flesh which is upon the earth" (Gn 9:9, 16).

THE IMPLICATIONS OF THE WORD

The relations between natural and supernatural revelation, between that given by the very being of things and that given by the word, and all the consequences in the spheres of natural truth (philosophy), natural ethics and law, etc. is one of the central problems in the controversy between catholic and protestant theologians—though of course the latter are not in accord (consider the discussion between Barth and Brunner, and Lackmann's statistical summary of the interpretations of Rom 1:18f); and catholics vary considerably in their interpretations of the Vatican definitions. It is not our intention to survey the problem in its entirety but rather to consider just one limited though essential aspect, one which may help to reconcile differences and allay prejudices. It is by no means a new aspect, being simply the application of the generally accepted christology to the problem of revelation; but perhaps it has not yet been adequately worked out in detail.

Once the older apologetic and fundamental theology had shaken off the imprecise ideas of german idealism, both philosophic and christian, according to which creation was simply identified with revelation or the manifestation of the divine being, and the revelation of the word, in all its

depth and force, seemed reduced to a mere stage in the utterance of creation itself, there began a period marked by
the emergence of a direct, and therefore naive, unreflective
dualism between the two forms of revelation: on the one
hand an independent revelation derived from the creation,
whose content could be detailed with some precision, even
though uncertainty remained about fallen man's capacity
for attaining knowledge in the religious sphere; on the other
the denial of any such "second" source of revelation alongside that of the word of God in Christ. This second source
seemed merely to tone down, obscure and distort the clear,
definitive and exhaustive word that the father willed to give
to the world through his son, since men then claimed to
derive most of what it concerned them to know simply from
nature—and to reserve for philosophy and ethics much that
derived from the word of God, almost to the point of sup-
planting it.

Surely this ostensibly catholic misconception, which oc-
casionally *seemed* to be adopted even by authorized ex-
ponents, is a clear indication of some defect in basic
principles. It is true that catholic theology has endeavored
to rise from the second period of simple dualism to a third
which would be characterized by a consistent and comprehensive christological outlook; but its consequences have
yet to strike our evangelical brothers as sufficiently forceful
and practical.

What follows is to be understood as an expression of a
christological outlook. It will not however adhere to the
usual course which starts from principles drawn from the
revelation in creation to arrive at the revelation in the word
as the crown and summit—a course many evangelical theo-

58

logians consider impossible as a method and at the least involving insuperable difficulties. Here we proceed in the reverse direction, from the revelation in the word to that in creation. This we do not on the basis of the well known if sparse texts of scripture, which speak of revelation in creation and whose meaning is the subject of considerable dispute, both philological and theological, but by determining what the word of revelation itself presupposes and implies. It may be that the resources of modern philology and psychology make us more amenable to this method than were our immediate predecessors. These sciences have taught us to discover, in an apparently uniform structure, different superimposed layers: philology by going back to "sources" and to previous redactions or verbal traditions, and thus, especially as regards texts of the old testament, coming upon certain archaic, legendary or mythical foundations; psychology by its parallel attempt to formulate the implications of the conscious spiritual life in the spheres of the instinctive, organic and vegetative life—processes which are at very early ages submerged into the twilight and total darkness of the unconscious. Yet this method did not have to wait for the coming of these two sciences. It was known from the very beginning of philosophical thought, and practiced as the method of "analytics," which is not only the title of Aristotle's book on logic (indicating the results of reflection on direct perceptions of the categories of being), but was the metaphysical method employed by Socrates and Plato, and later by neoplatonism in its ascent to God by way of reflection. Perhaps too it might be possible to read Hegel in this light (the reverse of the usual): to explain the "nothingness" of the pure hic et nunc we

59

must, by analysis, traverse all the stages of reality until we reach the divine ground. But we are not now engaged in philosophy, but in christian theology; and if, whatever its method and system, Christ is for it the summit and crown of all God's work in the world, if he is, as Paul and Irenaeus say he is, the anakephalaiosis of the entire creation, then theology's duty is to portray this in all its sublimity. This is its aim, and its means is an analysis of christology, bringing out the cosmic presuppositions that the incarnation of the word of God implies.

1

Our starting point is the "directness" of God's word as it encounters us in holy scripture. It could reasonably be objected that what comes to us most directly is not the scriptural word but the word in its living proclamation, which is essentially continuous with the word to which scripture is but a pointer, the word Jesus Christ who endowed the apostles with the office and charismatic power of preaching. This is true enough; yet the scriptural word has as its function to bear witness, under the inspiration of God, to the word of life, to the total Christ, both head and body. For this reason, and because it is word, in the human and primary sense (whereas that to which it bears witness can only be so described in a deeper and not directly intelligible sense), it is above all methodical and objective. Scripture is one book among many, or rather a collection of books of various kinds; moreover it is one of extreme complexity, posing more scientific problems that any other in world literature—one therefore that must be painstakingly examined philologically. We cannot agree with Origen (himself a great philologist!) when he equates the application of the tools of philology to scripture with a handing over of the incarnate word to the torturer. This implied identification of the scriptural word with the word himself and of the interpretation of scripture with the incarnation of the logos is so absolute as to lead to numerous false conclusions. Insofar as it expresses mistrust of anything to do with natural philology this ingenious theory is really an outcome of the alexandrian tendency toward the doctrine of one nature.

Nonetheless, after allowing due scope for the science of the word, we must acknowledge what is correct in Origen's view. Holy scripture, as the uniquely privileged witness to a unique event, is so intimately bound up with it that, apart from the event—understood in the sense in which it is witnessed in scripture, or witnesses itself in scripture—it cannot be interpreted at all. Philology can help toward this understanding but it can neither compel nor replace it. To understand the scriptural text according to its own defined mission (and to do otherwise would be to mistake its whole tenor) means accepting it on faith as the witness of the Holy Spirit (through the instrumentality of men) to yahweh's dealings with his chosen people of the covenant, and to the fulfilling of this covenant in the person of Jesus, God and man. It is true of course that in every human statement there is a gap between what it conveys and what it means to convey, the word holding them apart as well as conjoining them. Yet we can never postulate a unique word that should correspond with the uniqueness of what is meant, for the very reason that no event in the world can claim absolute uniqueness; there is always some point of comparison with other events, and so there is always something one event shares with another. Consequently, however personal and relatively original a given utterance may be, it always contains an element of generality and formality, bringing it within the purview of linguistics, grammar, syntax, poetics, comparative philology and so forth. What scripture bears witness to is, on the one hand, a section of human history, and thus something which can be expressed quite simply in human words. But scripture is also so unique in kind that there is an absolute limit fixed to its comparability with other events, and thus necessarily a clearly drawn limit to the application of philology to the word thus witnessing. If what it conveys is wholly unique then this uniqueness is the central, dominant factor in the statement designed to convey it. In other words this testifying word necessarily implies this content; and, if scripture is to be understood as essentially the word authorized by the Holy Spirit (since only God can speak adequately of God, only God can say what he means by his revelation), then it must be seen as the Spirit's word about the word that is the son; and this, its sublimest aspect, implies a relation to the trinity. This brings out the partial truth of what Origen says, namely that the distinction between the testifying word and the word testified to is an incomplete one. Large tracts of scripture do not merely relate the revelation made by Yahweh to his people through the intermediation of Moses, the kings, the prophets, even the pagans, and finally in the word that is Christ. They are themselves revelation. In the prayers of the psalmist the Spirit reveals what prayer means for God; the words of the prophets not only indicate a particular historical background, but the core of what God willed to speak is contained in the actual situation through the prophets. The sapiential books do not refer to any historical background but are themselves a tranquil contemplation of the historical revelation, and bring out, in the form of revelation, the goods therein contained. In the new testament the interaction is still more evident. This alone imparts to the words of scripture not only a unique value in themselves but also a peculiar resonance that carries to every generation and causes a great turbulence in the sea of human words. Something of the uniqueness of the object testified to inevitably belongs to the word that testifies, imparting to it its inner trustworthiness as witness. Something of the logic of the object testified to, above all the cross and the resurrection of Christ, colors the logic of the expression. This has been often noticed, but at the same time seems never to have been adequately treated.

2

The word of the Spirit, which is what scripture is, bears reference to the word of the father, which is the son. The word uttered by the church in her preaching, a word we directly encounter, originates in this word of the son, so much so that, in every detail, it refers back to it, represents and expounds it, and impresses it on the hearers. It permits of no independent, definitive sense of its own but, as with the church's liturgical sacrifice, only has meaning in relation to Christ's words, acts and being, a meaning brought about in obedience to him. Thereby we gain an unimpaired vision of the reality scripture means to convey as a living tradition (proclamation), and this reality, together with its implications, is the subject of the present study, namely the incarnate word of God. We may take as our point of departure Christ as word, that is, preacher and "prophet" of the father and of his kingdom. As such he implies straightaway the entire revealed word of history since Abraham, indeed since Noah and Adam, for inasmuch as he satisfies all justice, fulfills all the promises, his word, teaching and truth build up into a single whole all that God has shown forth and effected as truth relating to him. Likewise what is, according to his word, also a part of the revealed word can now only be understood as rounding off the exposition of his depth and height and breadth and length—we refer to the theologies of Paul and John, the Acts as the prototype of church history (to which belong the catholic epistles by way of completion), and the Apocalypse as the recapitulation of the whole old and new testament theologies of history. Further all that belongs to the church's official exegesis and every partial manifestation of the fullness of the word of Christ in individual charismatic missions—all this is a palpable result of the living power of the word exercised over the whole of history.

We only make mention of the historical dimension of the divine utterance in order to see how it centers on the word of Christ. For this indeed is a word spoken by a man to men, understandable by them as a human word, yet, in the opinion of those who heard, a word of one who spoke as no man ever spoke (Jn 7:46), who spoke "as one having power, and not as the scribes" (Mt 7:29). Wherein this power consisted he himself made known: in his being sent by the father, in his obedience to the father, so that what he taught was the echo of his father's teaching, and his whole life, the very flesh and blood that he had assumed, was through his obedience taken up into his word. His word transcended the temporal, reaching up both to God and to his own life; yet it belonged to the general human category, while being at the same time absolutely unique. Had it not come within that category it would not have been human at all, and the word would not have been made flesh. Nor would we be able to understand Christ's word in its special mode of transcendence. But we now see what it means for someone to stake his life for every utterance he dares to make, and to say that he means thereby a truth that surpasses his own relative existence and that is absolute. He may fall short of it either in understanding or conduct; still he means it, and he does not necessarily fail it. Yet the transcendence of Christ's word in reaching out to his own life and to his father has, with all its humanness, something setting it wholly apart, for to it alone the plenitude of authority was given by the father. Let us take as an example the parable of the unmerciful servant. Does the word here give us a similitude that, however, wholly transcends the category of similitudes because it springs from a reality already given and made visible by its means, a reality immanent within it? What gives it that force which attaches to every particular application but which is yet only present for one who assents to the reality signified as the basis of the narrative? What but precisely that fact, present behind it all, that Christ is the price paid for the redemption. Each of the words here spoken is, for its utterance to be made at all possible, covered with a warranty sealed in blood. The

65

utmost justice—to the point of delivering the unmerciful servant to the torturers (consider what this means, when God is king)—is also, since behind it lies Christ's sacrifice of body and blood, the adequate expression of the utmost mercy of God. We cannot interpret this story in merely human terms, merely ethically, nor, despite its severity, merely as "old testament" in tone. It must be accepted as told by Christ making his way toward the cross; in fact the verse that follows speaks of his return to Judea (Mt 19:1). The parable form is preserved and, at the same time, transcended. It is preserved insofar as there is a story with a formal correspondence between it and what it signifies; transcended because here the similitude does not indicate the reality, as is the case with poetic parables, but the reality directly points to itself in the similitude, creates its own breathing space. This transcendence is the despair both of philology and psychology. Both of these, relying on the doctrine of the incarnation, according to which everything belonging to Christ's human activities proceeds in a wholly human fashion, claim the existence of a sphere which, for the time being, is not transcended in favor of what is wholly unique. This sphere however does not exist, therefore both can only propound their judgments while they themselves are, at a deeper level, the objects of judgment. It is not as though they were not allowed to carry out their work to the end and then have to interrupt it at a certain point when the mystery begins. The mystery, for that matter, begins at the outset so that if they want to pursue their objects to the end no one stops them. The question is simply whether, once they realize that they are wholly subject to the judgment of the word, which they proposed to judge, they must begin all over again in faith.

Does this then mean a total collapse of scientific procedure, and imply that it is absurd to include theology as one of the faculties? Apprehending this conclusion theologians take refuge in a theory of "two storeys." On the lower level is the Jesus of history, exhaustively analyzed both philologically and psychologically, while on the upper storey is the word of Christ as son of the father, the object of faith, both communal and individual—as if there were in Christ anything comprehensible in human terms that was not to be interpreted, from the outset, in function of his divine mission. This methodic schizophrenia is the counterpart of the cleavage in the individual inquirer who, though believing, is still a sinner. But even so, it is inadmissible since what determines the method is not the inquirer but the object. This object is Christ whose word, if it is to be at all understood in its content and intention, comprises both the cross and his mission by the father. For the cross guarantees the truth of his words by the sacrifice of his own life, and the mission guarantees that his sacrifice is not that of a fanatic, but an act of obedience to a divine commission. We see that there is a connection between word, cross and commission that is of its very nature wholly unique, a logic thought out ad hoc, or better, ad hunc, and applying to this case alone but with ineluctable necessity. It is especially in John that the uniqueness of the logic of Christ's words comes out, formulated as it is in an almost abstractly scientific way. There we have presented a clear gradation between the primary proof of the truth of the word and a secondary, supplementary process. The former rests on the analytical connection between the truth of the word (for example "I

67

am the light of the world," "I am the resurrection") and the sacrifice of body and blood, both being understood as obedience to the father and as self-revelation of the father—a perception which leads directly to faith and which issues from faith in a mysterious, living identity. But if anyone, through some spiritual weakness, some resistance to the truth arising out of sin, lacks the power to follow this christological logic and to yield to its evidence, another way opens to him, one which is given first place in Christian apologetics—that of miracles and prophecy. This is the argument for belief in the uniqueness of the all fulfilling word in the son from the evidence of the relationship between promise and fulfillment, between the charisma proclaimed (prophecy) and the charisma manifested (miracle) (Lk 4:18). It accords with the logic of the redemptive process where, instead of dwelling on the unique character of the central feature and letting conviction follow from having seen the justness of its structure, we turn to the various factors connected with the preparation, the earlier stages and pointers; these can only be understood, individually as well as collectively, if interpreted as promises of something to come, and this is only possible after the fulfillment has taken place. The overwhelmingly clear proof which God bestows on those of lesser insight is the correspondence between the old testament and the new, a most remarkable thing, so wide and manifold as to be exemplified in countless instances. It is in virtue of the sovereignty of the son of God that he assigns this historical consideration to the second place. It is not his will to be argued to from premises outside himself, for he is the truth which bears all evidence in itself, and which is susceptible to no comparison

68

other than with itself. The whole economy of the two testaments consists in applying the essential truth of the incarnation to the whole range of human history; this is not just something accidental, exterior, made for apologetic purposes, a concession to human need. Consequently the first thing to be made clear is that the father has given all power to the son, and that what he fulfills, namely the promise, derives from him its persuasive force.

It is necessary to insist that, in addition, the perception of the "harmonies of the two testaments" (Charlier) is far superior, as a mode of comprehension, to the methods of philology and psychology, as these themselves show us (unfortunately, we may say) only too plainly. Whatever natural precondition is required for understanding *this* logic of revelation, it does not consist in a fine discrimination of philological minutiae, but rather in a feeling for form, a sense of the proportions of the whole, of the relative importance of detail, not only in regard to sensible but also to spiritual reality. The great spiritual writers who have made this the focal point of their theology—Irenaeus, Origen (with his enormous influence in both the east and the west), Augustine, Rupert, Pascal, Newman—all had this esthetic sense and outlook. Certainly this does not mean that it is possible to prescind from faith in cultivating a biblical esthetic productive of factual results. All it means is that God, for the understanding of the truths of faith, calls upon all the cognitive powers of man, and that the coarse-grained philology to which the old testament makes no appeal, as being "unmodern," is only dumb in its regard because of a want of sensibility.

The argument from Christ as manifested in scripture has,

69

all through history, both ecclesiastical and secular, refuted with a truly divine irony all the insidious suggestions of his enemies. It is so cogent because the recorded facts rule out the alternative: either son of God or else purely man of the highest religious perceptions. It compels this other alternative (as philology and psychology might propose): either son of God or else the hallucinatory invention of enthusiastic followers, God's son or psychopath. Anyone who thinks "religious genius" is a sufficient explanation has certainly not read the new testament objectively. All attempts to bring the unique figure of Christ within general laws miscarry; they fall back for an explanation on deception or mental disorder, as the Jews did once, and have always done (Mt 28:15; Jn 8:48).

3

We only need to contemplate the mystery of the union of the divine and human in Christ from the other aspect in order to perceive its entire implication. In Christ there is nothing human (we speak of course of the actus humani, not of the actus hominis) that is not the utterance and expression of the divine; and likewise there is nothing divine that is not communicated and revealed to us in human terms. This applies not only to all the acts of the public life, his preaching, founding of the church, passion and resurrection, but equally to his hidden acts, his prayer to the father, his obedience, his love for the father unto death. It is precisely this inner aspect that is most essential, definitive, in the whole economy of the redemption. For it is not true that the acts and states of the redeemer, by which he makes for redeemed humanity a new spiritual and heavenly home, are only partially human acts (that is to say, a subordinate part therefore), while those where the human nature as such falls short of the divine call for the intervention of the higher nature, that of the God-man. That would be pure arianism. The acts and states by which Christ redeems us are genuine human acts, from the lowest to the highest; and though they are never solely human they are always human. Scholasticism, for purposes of classification, confines the idea of "religio" to certain bounds; but once we free it from these and set it in the light of the adoration to be given in spirit and truth, self-surrender in faith, hope and charity, everything by which Christ signifies his love to the father and to men is an actus religionis.

These acts then, as we have just emphasized, are not to be exhaustively explained by derivation from the "abstract" nature, man. At the same time it is obvious that, despite the uniqueness of Christ as divine and human, they are still acts of a man who to be man must fall within the range of the "abstract" term man. Consequently there is no question of applying to Christ a definition which would distinguish him as man essentially from other men, setting him apart for instance as "man *for* his fellowmen," as opposed to "us others" who are only "men *with* our fellowmen." In any case such an account of what Christ and other men are respectively only brings out the specifically social, horizontal function of human nature, prudently omitting its relation to God; and besides, it makes, if we examine the argument closely, Christ and the rest of men share a common nature only analogously, not univocally. The "ordinary," "normal"

71

man is a self-contained person, and this fact confines his relationship with his fellowmen to certain limits. He cannot be their representative before God, still less offer himself as a sacrifice for them, or feed them with his own substance, his flesh and blood. Christ's humanity on the other hand is, from the outset, a function of his divine person and so a fit instrument for all those acts which are required for the redemption of mankind. Because of this, and since in spite of all Christ's humanity must be designated a pure humanity, it could well be maintained that the rest of men become, in Christ, competent as regards acts to which they are not fitted by their own human nature. The above-mentioned theology of man fails, on a decisive point, to take full account of the incarnation. In becoming man Christ falls into the universal category of man, and so Paul's expression "found as a man" (Phil 2:7) implies an identity of nature persisting, regardless of the analogy conveyed by the κένωσις, even in the greatest of his acts as God-man; and in this precisely consists the taking of man's nature into the unity of the God-man in order to redeem it. It certainly follows that the acts of Christ—being acts of his human nature, and therefore insofar as the man Christ manifests his "religio" toward the father in adoration and obedience during his agony in the garden—are truly acts of natural religion. They are not merely natural religion, but this is no reason for denying that they are *also* natural religion; it does mean that we have both the right and the duty to affirm natural religion as necessarily implied in christology. Were this not so then the "religio" of Christ must have seemed supernatural in a way inconsistent with the ordinariness, lowliness and accessibility he showed in his human relations. He must

72

have seemed quite other than those quasi-divine wise men and religious founders in his capacity for acts beyond ordinary human nature. Then his summons could only have involved a misconception, and the twelve, on being asked "Will you also go?" would have had to withdraw—at any rate after his promise to make his flesh and blood the food of all, a thing absolutely supernatural. Of course they did not dream of "imitating" him in such incomprehensible acts, nor did he demand that they do the exact same thing as he. Nonetheless he did not intend their following of him to be no more than a mirroring of his acts in a different sphere, one appropriate to *their* humanity. He meant it to be a real identification with him, and this despite all the emphasis he laid on the uniqueness of his sonship. This is what we now have to consider.

When we say that Jesus, as man, performs the acts of religion the expression as man means that he does so not only as exemplar but as a model, not only as filius unicus but as primus inter filios pares. This implies that the act of religion is an act of man as such, apart from which it would be impossible to understand either the incarnation or the redemption. It would amount to losing sight of man's elevation through Christ to community with the divine nature, were Christ as exemplar to be emphasized to the detriment of him as model, or the equality of nature stressed to the point of forgetting the uniqueness of his sonship, which predestines him, in an altogether different way from Adam, to be the head of mankind and makes him draw all things (Jn 12:32) in heaven and earth (Eph 1:10) into his unique status (visibly expressed in his being raised up on the cross).

73

The elevating, transforming and creative power of the gratia capitis is so great that, between the religio appropriate to human nature as such and that offered to man through the grace of redemption, the only relation is one of analogy; any relation less than this is inadmissible. And though human nature was impaired by sin still, despite all its disastrous consequences, *this* analogy is not annulled. All it means is the inhibition (seen constantly in the individual) of an ever-present essential function. No other interpretation of the guilt persisting in mankind is possible.

The analogy between natural and revealed religion is conceived correctly and in accordance with what revelation itself tells us only on two conditions. We must neither deny the existence of natural religion nor see it as self-contained and sufficient. It must be taken, according to the intention of the creator of the natural order, as of its very nature an initial stage. This means that God, in the order of creation, truly began what he was to perfect in the order of Christ's redemption; began, that is to say, in the sense of establishing an enduring initial stage wherein what is begun does not imply a reaching beyond itself (*a* desiderium naturale visionis, sive efficax sive inefficax), nor (what comes to the same thing) claim to be understandable only when raised to the order of grace. Neither is its incorporation into the final synthesis to be held dependent on its essence being considered merely as a "promise" of something of a higher order. Such conceptions would impair and even exclude the freedom of grace as God's self-revelation to the creature, God's freedom to enter into a covenant with a people chosen at his discretion. To speak of continuity between the two orders is in fact highly misleading and, sooner or later, involves making grace (even as medicinalis) an epiphenomenon of nature.

We can speak of "implication" in this connection only in the sense of nature (that is, human nature) being taken into a mode of being it cannot attain of itself—since this mode is divine and unique and thus only accessible through Christ, God and man—without having to be completed in its own order, its "substantiality," as regards a missing part—namely religion. Nature possesses a predisposition for this superadded mode by reason of its inchoate character. This character however does not consist in a platonist longing after grace and the vision of God, a longing that includes a latent claim to these. Nor is this predisposition a constant attitude of resignation and indifference to what is to come on the ground that no one can see into the divine counsels. What it means is active readiness, the expression of the true essence of creatureliness, for every possible initiative on the part of God's will without at the same time anticipating it. This readiness was taken up and fulfilled by Christ, which shows exactly what analogy here means.

We cannot conclude this line of thought without exhibiting the analogy as one of personality and so of the uniqueness of the individual. Uniqueness enters into the very essence of man, so much so that it must be taken into consideration even when we view him in the abstract. So it was that Hegel was obliged to find room in his metaphysics for history in the concrete; and only so was it possible for the only-begotten of the father to become a

man among men. And in him the uniqueness of each individual rises superior to its precarious situation in time,
and so attains to the "father's house" and the co-inheritance.

4

Now at last we can profitably consider another implication,
already alluded to in section 2, namely the christian and
ecclesiastical existence implied in that of Christ. This subject, like all others broached here, is far too extensive to
be treated fully; we must be content to indicate its place
in the general ensemble. If the relationship between nature
and grace, as seen from the aspect of the incarnation, almost defies expression in rational terms, this is even more
the case here. Previously it was a question of seeing one
reality being imparted through a higher one in such wise
that the latter, in its sovereign freedom, bestows a mode of
being, a selfness, to which the self as nature has no claim;
yet this self had from the outset been formed in view of
this new being. Now we are concerned with how God's
word in Christ arranges a participation in himself in such
a way that the participator thereby realizes himself at the
deepest level of his being, attains self-knowledge in the
unique relationship of member to head. The similes of head
and members, of vine and branches, are taken from the
natural, subspiritual order and so are only pointers to the
reality, not the reality itself. The members and branches
have their own personality and responsibility for their acts,
and thus are bound by ethics and religion. Their obliga-
tions are by no means superseded by reason of the event

represented by the two similes, nor through the supervention of the order of sin and its debilitating effects. We are concerned here not so much with the latter as with the accord between ethical and religious ideals and the soteriological fact: what the christian is obliged to bring about is granted him by Christ as already effected, without however removing the necessity for striving after perfection. What this means is most clearly seen in the special case of the apostles. They were entrusted with the word of God, with proclaiming not the bare word but the word along with its characteristic powers. The authority to speak included the messianic power to work miracles, as if to show that this conjunction of word and deed was not the specific mark of Christ who alone, in virtue of being sent by the father, could equate his existence with the mission received. The disciples received something of this identity by communication from him, and not merely something after the fashion of the credentials given to the prophets of the old testament. The holiness attributed by Paul to the faithful is not that of the synagogue, but a participation of that of Christ, their head. His death and resurrection, as an accomplished fact, was the grace communicated to them, and this primary grace of Christ became the ethical ideal they were called to realize subsequently. Peter received the office of feeding Christ's flock which, because it is Christ's, can only rightly, that is, in Christ's way, be fed by Christ, in whom the priest-shepherd and lamb-victim are one and the same. This is why, immediately after, there followed the prophecy of Peter's following to the death of the cross; an express "follow thou me" is appended to the gift of this conjoined function of Christ (Jn 21:19, 22). This special case of the

77

apostolic office in the church throws light on that of the ordinary believer, also sent to live the life of the word. What differentiates Christ and Peter is not for a moment neglected. In fact the lord of the church stresses it to the utmost, and thus brings out all the more strongly the paradox of the christological unity so entrusted to him. Furthermore the theological paradoxes of the relationships between Peter and John, between authority and charity in the church, brought out at the end of John's gospel, are contrasted (admittedly only in the catholic interpretation) almost to the point of making them at variance. Nonetheless the effect is not one of fragments lying lifeless and apart, as in the paradoxes of Pascal, Kierkegaard and Dostoevsky, but of elements bound together by the head into a formal unity, one of supreme beauty, the beauty of the new testament bridal church, realized in Mary and every true case of sanctity. It is a unity free of the tortured complications of human dialectic, possessing the simplicity and directness of the attitude "Behold the handmaid of the lord." So perfect is its simplicity as to be almost equated with the human ideal, which indeed it is, but only because it is conceived by God and bestowed by the son.

Here it is well to remember that being human cannot be expressed simply in the abstract ethical formula "self-perfection in freedom." This striving is inseparable from man's organic nature, whose laws operate in the direction of freedom, though they must be acknowledged and admitted in the patience befitting a created being. It was not in climbing the steep path to "self-perfection" that Mary became a mother, but in self-surrender to God's direct will and to the disposition intrinsic to her womanly nature and to what took flesh within it. In this way the fruitfulness of her faith was conjoined with that of her womb and of her whole being. This shows us how Luther's conception of the act of faith was somewhat restricted in comparison with the older german and christian accounts wherein the element of surrender and loyal discipleship, the human in other words, was far more prominent than in the protestant dialectic of sin and grace. If this human factor is not seen as implicit in the holiness of the church the "naked" soteriological dialectic only too easily reduces faith to an academic abstraction.

5

The last implication we wish to mention (without trying to reach any systematic conclusion) requires, for complete acceptance, a much more thorough exposition; an abbreviated account is almost inevitably misleading. The history of God's dealings with man is wholly centered in Christ, from whom it radiates into two periods of time; starting from him we gain an understanding of all that is disposed in view of him and all that proceeds from and through him.[1] Christ himself often indicated this implication of all that was ordained in view of salvation (Jn 5:46–47; 8:52–58; Mt 22:41–45) and, having accomplished his own part and risen again, expounded it to the infant church for forty days (Lk 24:44f). For Paul this implication is identical with the mystery whose servant he has become, and for

[1] I would refer the reader to my *A Theology of History*, New York 1963.

the author of the apocalypse it is once again the dramatic meaning of world history. In fact when we speak here of world history we must include a further, and necessary, implication of the whole history of man in the history of salvation. This implication is only too familiar in one way, and yet when examined closely appears a very strange one. Of course we see Christ as the head elevated above all history who will come again to pass judgment on the living and the dead, and so over the whole course of history. But this hope of ours is wholly eschatological; the gospel admonishes us to watch and persevere in prayer rather than to set about theologizing history. The meaning of history is so dependent on the mind of the creator and judge that we cannot determine it in advance.

Yet, since the word was made flesh, the various histories comprised in that of Christ himself, that of the covenant with Israel, the course followed out by God with his people, all belong, as history, to the content of revelation. The whole patristic and medieval theology of history is based on the idea that the different stages, up to Abraham, from Abraham to Moses, from Moses to the judges and to David, from David to the prophets, from the prophets to post-exilic Israel, and from that time to Christ, were actually a progressive revelation; so much so that these stages were taken, in summary fashion, to pertain not only to sacred history but also world history in general. The ordo et gradus in profectu mundi, spoken of so frequently and in such detail by Bonaventure and other great scholastics, was derived from their view of sacred history, but it was also connected with their philosophical reflection on the possible meaning of the general course and progress of history. They saw this as a processus ab imperfecto ad perfectum consisting of 1) the eliciting of free acceptance from mankind of the salvation freely given (and so the eliciting of Mary's assent from each successive generation); 2) a corresponding inner understanding of and cooperation with God's plan of salvation together with a longing for its fulfillment, which is elicited from the witnesses, both explicit and implicit, and figures of the old testament; 3) an ever deeper embodying of grace in the world in its historical course, so as to penetrate it in its own created being and guide it to its true home, and so to attain to the incarnation of God— Deus cum limo—the integritas universi (see *Breviloquium* 4, fourth ed, Quar 5, 244).

It may be objected that this theology of history is necessarily confined to the time of the old testament, the only time when the great stages of salvation could coincide with the different epochs of world history, and that, once the fullness and end of the times are reached in Christ, any subsequent interpretation along these lines of the stages of history is impossible and superfluous. It is true that the older theologians made the whole course of world history fit into the chronology of the bible, and saw the eschatological consciousness of the new testament as an awaiting and experiencing of the last, the seventh period of time, the time of Christ, as a brief coda to the preceding. But our consciousness of history extends so much further in both directions that the old idea of world history implied in the history of the incarnation of the word is no longer relevant. So nowadays it is the archeologists (Albright) and culture philosophers studying the near east who assure us that we must not just give up the whole project. Un-

81

hampered by the doubts and inhibitions of the theologians, they approach the whole question from the opposite end, from the angle of secular history, and ask what part the bible plays in the two millennia before Christ, so decisive for the spiritual development of mankind. All that precedes them is but a vast, uncoordinate series of events, of hardly more than biological significance, preceding the real history of culture. What follows is hardly more than the logical outcome of the premises laid down in that period; for it was during those two millennia that the spirit broke through and allowed of the formation of higher cultures and their social structures, their political, religious and esthetic myth; and from these essential prerequisites there finally emerged the birth of abstract ideas, and so of liberty of thought and of the universality of spiritual understanding in the Greek world. It was this period, so decisive for the human destiny of mankind (what Jaspers calls the "axis period") that the historical articulation of the divine revelation occurred, on the one hand pursuing its course in sovereign independence, quite apart from the political and religious designs of the great nations all around, and on the other not simply rejecting this world of culture but reckoning with it and adapting it. "Moses was instructed in all the wisdom of the Egyptians" (Acts 7:22); the cultural influence of Mesopotamia and Syria on the thought and categories of the bible need not be emphasized.

The question thus arises, decisive for our subject, whether the historical development that took place in the sphere of the biblical revelation has any sort of inner relationship to the contemporary development in the near eastern culture within which the minute state of Israel was embedded.

82

There is no question here of deriving the "progress" in the religious sphere from that in the secular, or of simply proving them parallel. Yet we have to ask whether the clearly visible steps by which the spirit of biblical revelation—in contrast to the rigid conservatism of the Jews—in its own fashion emerges on the plane of the incarnation, form a process having no real bearing on the steps by which the spirit of the world advances from one level of understanding to another until it reaches the plane of a universal human culture in Greece. The question suggests itself more readily if we do not ascribe the biblical revelation and its gradual development solely or even primarily to God acting from outside and above, but rather to the growth of real understanding among the jewish people of the spiritual consequences arising from a vital religious element present since the time of Abraham and Moses. There is no reason to regard this question and a possibly affirmative answer as an encroachment of liberalism into theology. It is in fact simply the extension, only now made possible, of one of the central aspects of patristic and scholastic theology, and more profoundly a necessary outcome of christology in its fullest sense. For the history of the human race, into which the redeemer inserts himself, is not divided into two clearly separate and distinct histories. There is only one history, that of man from paradise to the last day, and its significance is not exhausted in the fact of Adam's fall and the eschatological redemption through Christ. Nor does the divine seed implanted in world history, there to "die and rise again," wish to establish its own second history alongside the first, but rather to propagate salvation in the one and only history. Let it suffice here only to note this con-

83

clusion and its necessity, though it still requires a great deal of elaboration and analysis. We simply propound a thesis without fully exploring the grounds which support it, but we do so in view of the implications of the word which, in their interaction, seem to lead to this conclusion. Theology of course cannot, in hegelian fashion, reach a full clarification of the meaning of world history, which would make Christ's judgment superfluous. But it can reach the decisive conclusion that if secular history in its temporal ramifications is proved to be of real consequence in the biblical sphere, it cannot, in its secular meaning, be indifferent as regards sacred history, for it has *in its totality* been impregnated through and through by the word.

A similar relationship holds good between the categories (we might say the archetypes) of the natural religious reason and the biblical teaching of the living God and the unique redeemer of mankind. This was brought out with increasing force from Justin and the Alexandrians up to Eusebius, from whose time it was never lost to view. A purely passive "hearing reason" is self-contradictory; thus man's thought of God, even when allowance is made for the excessive presumption of reason tainted by original sin, cannot persist without some rudimentary system in which it tries to represent the relations between God and man in the events of history. What happens perforce is that the word of God, in replacing the false gods, condemns and indeed scorns the material content of man's ideas of the Godhead, but nonetheless takes over for its own use the bare framework, and thus, on occasion, even preserves (in the economy of grace) something of the content. Why should the sapiential books and the epistle to the Hebrews

84

not employ the language and modes of thought of platonist cosmology and theology to reveal the truth of what Plato dimly envisaged? Why should Paul not use the language of those whom he addressed in explaining the mystery of Christ to the Ephesians or the Colossians? To his mind it was only necessary to see the myth of these jewish gnostics aright, that is, in the critical light of the actual events of the life of Christ, in order to make clear that it too had some intimation of the truth. At the same time he held that Christ's redemptive acts must be seen in the light of the myth for only then does one aspect of the truth emerge, namely that the law, its enmity, the crushing of this enmity by Christ, all had a cosmic scope, affecting in other words the whole universe of being; that these are not merely moral but ontological phenomena. Such is Schlier's interpretation of the mind of Paul, and he goes on to say: "Formally and basically, what Paul's interpretation of the gnostic ideas amounts to is their adaptation to the apostolic message. This process of continual reinterpretation carried out, consciously, in the apostolic mind, indeed in christian thought generally, is a sign of a consistent essential correspondence in the objective order. For why should we not be allowed to do as regards the gnostics what is accepted as regards the Jews? Probably we have here a latent dogmatic prejudice. . . ." (*On Eph* 133).

Furthermore why should John not pour out the content of his singular visions into the mold of contemporary apocalyptic speech? This is what the catholic epistles did in large measure, and what Christ himself did not scorn to do. It is not just a matter of literary form, a choice of one rather than another equally good, as a comparison with the

85

texts of the Torah makes clear; but this is no reason to treat the matter shamefacedly. For it should not be too difficult to ascertain the correct mean between a theology which admits the necessity of myth on the grounds that sinful reason cannot do other than construct idols, and so be unable to discard them in its theology, and a liberal theology which fails to attribute to God's word the final judgment in the confrontation. A theology that discards natural judgment cannot escape it, since the bible is about natural religion. Such a theology may attempt to relegate it to the forecourts of philology and archeology, tamen usque redibit. But we may then be thankful for the difficulty of the problem which sends us, when we tire of philosophizing, back again to look at the theology of the bible.

86

God Speaks as Man

Through the liturgy the priest makes contact only with catholics, and among them only with the small number of those practicing. The liturgy has now become the preserve of an elite; and since we intend to show here the close bond between liturgy and preaching, liturgy and scripture reading, it may seem that real contact with the word must be confined to this narrow, esoteric circle. If so we would be approximating, where the liturgy is concerned, to the disciplina arcani of the fathers, and so instilling in the people the idea that the word establishes for itself a sacred sphere to which access is given only to the practicing believer.

This conclusion—no product of the imagination, but one to which the present situation actually tends—is accompanied by an attitude of resignation which runs counter to the true nature of the christian way of life. Christianity does not admit of any partiality or easily drawn frontiers; its impulse is always toward development and universalism. Esoterism is often the outcome of a psychological state of disquiet and fear. To combat this state—often disguised as a concern for the sacred—it is essential to examine fearlessly the supernatural revealed truths of christianity in the light of the sciences that have man as their object; these include philology, sociology and psychology. God, in becoming man and taking man into his trinitarian life, did no violence to human nature; in founding a new community centered on his incarnation it was not in spite of the laws of sociology, and religious sociology in particular. Consequently it cannot be disputed that the "religion" we contend to be the only true one is in one of its aspects on the same sociological plane as "other" religions. The bible is *the* sacred book but it is one among other sacred books, for each religion has its own. And every religion not only has its own liturgy but its practitioners endeavor to adduce in support of even the slightest religious observances a formal declaration of its will on the part of the Godhead. This general law is exemplified in the priestly code, which refers temple worship in all its details to the express instructions of Moses, even to the supernatural vision of the heavenly sanctuary he received on the holy mountain (Ex 25–31, 40). Likewise each religion has its own tendency to esoterism. These are not just vague similarities but the outcome of a fundamental trait persisting in human nature everywhere. Nor should they cause us apprehension. Rather we should be glad, for they furnish evidence for the true incarnation, the "humanization" of God.

When God becomes man then man as such becomes the expression, the valid and authentic expression of the divine mystery. Certainly man needs supernatural faith to understand what God in his sovereign freedom wills to proclaim in his spontaneous self-revelation. All the same this divine meaning is never something external and alien to man, who is indeed elected to be its expression. God is love. This he has testified to us as man, and so the two commandments of love can and must, in Christ, coalesce into one. In other words God, in revealing his own countenance to man, has also disclosed to him his own human countenance. God is under no sort of necessity to make use of man for his own self-revelation; but once he has decided on this and done so in an incarnation, all human dimensions, known and unknown, are taken up and used to express the absolute person. Consequently the christian religion, though it is from the sociological point of view but one among others, must necessarily embrace the totality of human nature; only thus can it be acknowledged as truly catholic.[1]

Humanism within christianity is indeed the central theme of our time, one which occupies the minds of all. It is the question above all others which the laity is most concerned with in its dialogue with nonchristian and nonpracticing brethren. At a time when the unity of the world is in the process of taking shape it is a problem calling for a comprehensive and bold solution. Paradoxically it comes to meet us as a consequence of the stirring biblical discoveries of recent years. Let us dwell on these for a moment.

The analogies between revealed religion and its neighboring cultures have, in our own day, come sharply to light and more and more points of dependence are evident. Much that previously seemed purely supernatural we now see as part of mankind's collective religious inheritance. On the other hand it is precisely these discoveries that have given

---

[1] This statement is not inconsistent with the fact that the universalist tendency we claim for revealed religion has itself a sociological aspect. Every religion (especially if it is grounded on revelation) must necessarily lay claim to universality and uniqueness. We can never isolate, in the religion of Christ, its divine and supernatural uniqueness from the universality which implies its extension to the whole human sphere.

89

us a better understanding of the mysteries of revelation. Perhaps today we understand better the mystery of Israel than did the christians of the past, better too the apostolic age in its jewish and hellenistic environment. The more clearly we discern the concrete and historical reality the more does revealed truth in all its profundities open itself to our view; in this we perceive one of the great antignostic laws, a law of the incarnation. The more Christ shows himself as in solidarity with every human word, every human act and thought, the more clearly he stands out from them as unique, as he who comes from above, empowered (without thereby being liable to the charge of madness or blasphemy) to utter the unheard-of words that no other man could venture: "Which of you shall convince me of sin?" "My words shall not pass away," "The son of man will come on the clouds of heaven . . ."

Let us look at the problem in the simplest way possible. To understand how far God has gone in using human ways of speaking, the structure of the latter must first be outlined; an understanding of this involvement however presupposes that we know what it expresses, namely a human experience. We treat therefore first of human experience, second of human speech, and third of the eternal word, incarnating itself in a man speaking in order to transform the man himself into a divine utterance.

1

What is the specific form that human experience takes?[1]
Man is essentially an historical being. His spirit comes to its
fullness in time, in a single, irreversible curve that leads
him through an uninterrupted succession of states, childhood, youth, maturity and age, though no one of these can
assure attainment of the next. There is a definite logic in
this sequence, though as Paul reminds us a certain alogical
element is involved: death; time, as a rushing toward a
final catastrophe, contains an element of futility, of nothingness, but this element itself is contained in a higher logic
of grace in that God leans down over the abyss for which
the creature, not the creator, was responsible. This only
intensifies the sharp, searing pain of our existence; every
stage of life, every situation requires that we let go of it
and transcend it. Yet each signifies for us a gift that never
returns, something that mirrors the absoluteness of eternal
duration. Maturity can never replace or even contain
within itself the vision of the world that is disclosed to the
fresh gaze of the child, at a time when the world was all
new, something innocent, paradisal, full of marvels, supernatural and natural at once, so that everything was possible,
everything near to God. The longing for irrecoverable
childhood is not just romantic: it can also have, as Péguy
and Bernanos have shown, a deep christian basis. In fact
the christian miracle consists in regaining the fullness of

[1] We are concerned here with the form, since within the limits of
an essay we cannot enter into the content of this experience, the
existent with its background of being in general, or into the dimensions
of the spirit in its knowledge of itself and others.

91

temporal duration. Entering the church through the gates of baptism is a fresh entry upon paradise, only available to children, by the "little way" which permits us to "redeem" the failure of time past. This christian miracle does not destroy the historical nature of man: non destruit naturam. The losses associated with time as nonentity are not eliminated, and only inasmuch as both, seemingly contradictory, aspects are lived out do the christian life and its experience of childhood recovered in growing old come to fulfillment.[1]

Man however is not just a child. Youth comes with its enthusiasms, fears and despondencies, the first experience of man's hidden depths, along with the tragic moment when a call is heard and the man, though apparently too young, makes his life's choice of a vocation and status in a moment that never recurs—a great gain but also a great loss. Choice presupposes freedom, but also hope, trust, surrender. Faith, hope and love appertain to man, and so also does the act of self-surrender in his maturity, of self-sacrifice for a duty, of finding the whole in the part. It belongs to him to experience the joy and the venture of responsibility and even the bitter consolations of failure, which show him that he is not a being apart but one among his fellows. Every one of his states offers the same view into the future, and the same striving to embody in a single whole his ceaseless flight toward the future. Thus the present becomes a qualitative synthesis of the whole of time, and is characterized by the ever-changing relationships between past and future.

Time then is by no means a uniform flux. It has moments of mysterious import, heights where man attains freedom

[1] See the very stimulating book by Jean Mouroux, *The Christian Experience*, New York 1954.

92

for himself. In his best moments he encounters his true image, his vocation and the grace it brings. If he accepts the duty placed before him that moment fills his time like a continuous moving present, and gives it a coherent, significant structure; but if he rejects it all that time has built for him will be lost. Faith, hope, love, this is what constitutes the existential form of the spirit in time, and every attempt to understand one's life must start from the fact that, outside the "little child hope" (Péguy) that lies between surrender in faith and the love that gives and loses itself, we have nothing to expect. Any attempt to pass beyond the glory and misery of "these three" (tria haec)—which is what every nonchristian religion strives after—only leads to an unprofitable gnosticism.

The life of peoples follows a similar logic. What they are they can only understand by looking at themselves in the light of the future and by using their memory of the past as a mirror. The measurable portion of their existence, their past history, gives a certain justification to their future; they see in their past certain points of comparison, promises in part fulfilled. And since this section of their lives yields a certain, however fleeting meaning the hope that all races of men have a hidden collective meaning in time may not be wholly illusory.

This law, valid for all peoples, is applicable to history in general since no man's or people's future and past can escape involvement with the destiny of mankind as a whole. For this very reason it applies of necessity to sacred history as the sum total of the dialog between God and his chosen people. Surely there must be present in the bible what the fathers call the "diastema" of our existence, the fundamen-

93

tal polarity and nonidentity of our experiences, the transition from one standpoint to the other. God himself has taken on the glory and humiliation of temporal existence; thus it is impossible to abstract the form of temporality from revealed truth for the sake of clinging to a barren system of timeless truth.

Let us recall one or two outstanding examples. Osee speaks of the days "when Israel was a child." What a feeling of homesickness is conveyed in the phrase! Here we have a tender recollection of childhood, not merely of a paradisal, prehistorical time but of one which really was, when all was fresh, pure and perfect in the relations between Israel and its God.

If there was no remembrance of a lost origin how could mankind hark back to it constantly through all the vicissitudes of history? Had there been no Abraham's grave in the promised land how could his descendents have let themselves be led by God to turn their backs on the fertile land of Egypt and to plunge into the desert of Sinai? Some of the psalms keep the memory of the original grace of the exodus so fresh that the episodes connected with the conclusion of the covenant are never mentioned. It is still the time of pure grace; the law is not yet. And when they do speak of the tremendous event of the covenant made before the flaming mountain, in the blood poured out between the people and the altar, and of the absolute commitment then first engaged, they present the law itself as grace, as something of absolute truth and strength, something necessary and possible to man.

This vivid sense of Israel's origins was no dream or myth, however much it might have become overladen in later years with nostalgia and sorrow. But we must see how remote it is from the theology of Deuteronomy, of Judaism and finally of Paul if we are to gain some notion of the inevitable decline of an idea and an ideal. For in the meantime a thousand years of experience of sin had intervened; Sion had been unfaithful, not only in isolated acts from which she could have recovered, but habitually, irretrievably. Could the law be kept at all? Did it in fact spring from God, or from some kind of intermediate being? It may well be good "in itself" but is it good "for me?" The pivot on which the whole of experience should revolve had been to some extent displaced in the time of the kings and prophets, and fully so during the time of the exile, of the sapiential and apocalyptic books. Much patience is needed if we are to assign both their absolute and relative value to all the experiences recorded in sacred history for in their very diversity they condition one another. The changing standpoint of different situations must be taken into account if each of them is to be understood, but the change of standpoint is itself ambiguous. On the one hand temporal existence is to be understood in relation to the future, like a book whose pages we turn as we read, so that the final synthesis, Paul's and John's conception of Christ, is something more perfect and comprehensive than, say, the ideas contained in the Pentateuch. At the same time every temporal accretion entails, infallibly, a definite loss. There are parts of the old testament which have greater force and life in themselves than in their new testament application and conception, and Christ insistently turns the minds of his followers back to these origins, so powerful in their workings and so fundamental.

95

We see then how a human law applies to sacred history and to its record in the bible. A present experience can only have truth and validity if conjoined with a definite vision and insight into the past and the future, with our central ideas framed within the memory, which serves as a guideline. The bible is full of this kind of projection into its own historical past; and in its absence the bible does not contain a full human truth—on the other hand it is not impaired by the inevitable gaps in the exposition.

It would be easy enough and even incorrect to allege that the Jews had constructed their own past and prehistory on the lines of their much later experiences, and that the scholar's duty is to separate the real facts of their origins from the general compound of fable and truth. On the contrary is should be admitted that the writers of the time of the kings and the great prophets and in the "fiery trial" of the exile could be wholly trusted to interpret the history objectively, to give the true sense of past events, which could well be understood better by those who came after than by those who had lived through them. The more Israel learned in faith to know and hope for the final goal of the future, the more clearly did the original point of departure appear through the images of its historic and fabled past.

It is perfectly in accord with the structure of human truth that an historic past (not a kind of myth to be demythologized) should, through the images projected (as in the story of paradise and the accounts of the patriarchs), guide a people toward its future, and that an early intuition of and encounter with the living God such as no other people experienced should have determined the historical, messianic and eschatological future of Israel.

Thus the truth of the bible can only be grasped in the context of a whole life's course. Unexpectedly we here come up against the old spiritual and catholic interpretation of scripture. Each sentence contains overtones of the whole; each word bears reference to the whole. The individual text itself can be seen passing through the successive stages and experiences they contain. Thus it has been proved that certain episodes of patriarchal times and even earlier were uprooted, wholly or in part, from their original life setting and inserted into the context of new religious experiences by the yahwists or one of their successors. Another example is Psalm 21, which may have been composed by one of yahweh's oppressed followers in the circle round Jeremias. It was then taken over into liturgical use, where the personal note of hope for liberation was given a social and universal significance, until finally, through the wonderful later addition which refers the whole purport of the text to the future, it gained its messianic application. The individual calling to his God becomes the oppressed people, who in turn become the oppressed at the end of time, embodied in the figure on the cross, expiring with this psalm on his lips.

These various relationships and correspondences elicited with the passage of time do not impair the truth of the bible. On the contrary it was the divine word that took hold of them as a definite proof of its truth. And truth of a living thing always lies in its totality. A man in making a definite choice sees himself confronted by the question: are you, in acting thus, being true to your first vision and your ultimate hope? Are you in accord with your highest self? In the same way God's sharp, piercing word to Israel is

97

always necessarily bound up with the past and the future. It creates history in that it produces *in* it the truth. It not only promises the future but exhibits it through the fulfill-ments already brought about. The logic of the vertical im-pingement of God's word on history must necessarily also be a logic that uses the life of the people for the purpose of its attaining justification.[1]

This is particularly evident in the relationship of the two testaments which, for the biblical personages, for Christ himself and for the fathers of the church was always con-sidered the fundamental, inexhaustible proof of the truth of God's word. But the great correspondence of the two testaments is only the supreme instance among countless other relationships and similarities and reproductions, such as those between the pre- and postmosaic religion, between the law and the prophets, between institution and event, between the historical and the sapiential books, between secular history and apocalyptic vision, between the gospel and apostolic or church history. The old testament as a whole and not only in isolated, apparently messianic texts was prophetic of the new, just as Christ and the apostles continually refer to the old law in order to vindicate there-by the whole range of effects produced by the incarnation.

Intermittently scripture seems to give the impression of deliberate inconsistency, of apparent inconsequentiality, so

[1] The supreme example, the annunciation to Mary, the queen of patriarchs and prophets, is also the clearest. The mystery of the divine decree is thrice proclaimed in an abrupt, vertical fashion (Lk 1:28,31, 35), and then inserted in the horizontal course of sacred history, whereby for Mary the absolute obedience demanded of her becomes comprehensible in human terms (Lk 1:32–35,36). There too we have the eschatological aspect (1:33), as also the revelation of the life (1:28, the father; 31, the son; 35, the Spirit).

as to make us see that certain words and episodes derive from very remote sources, are susceptible to a wealth of interpretations and manifold applications.[1] No work in the whole literature of the world has, even from the human standpoint, such a prodigious perspective as the bible. A single utterance echoes a hundredfold. Centuries of religious experience grew up around it before a single word came to us, and ceaseless meditation has, in response to the infinity of the divine word, come to endow even its human organ with a kind of corresponding infinity. From this we see that tradition in great part must antedate scripture. Scripture records and completes the living history of the revelation which comes to pass in man's experience of God.[2]

From this a further conclusion follows. The fathers of the church, along with Paul and the evangelists, saw the old testament almost exclusively as a prelude to the new, something essentially imperfect to be superseded by the coming revelation, and this quite apart from Israel's rejection of the messiah, by which it ceased to be the people of God. But we must not forget that Christ came to fulfill the millenary religious experience of the jewish people. In him continued to live the faith of the fathers of Israel, and

[1] In this connection we come up against the old controversy about the plurality of the senses of scripture. Gerhard von Rad in his commentary on Genesis (Philadelphia 1961) brings out convincingly how the yahwist, in adopting a new order for recording the various occurrences and experiences, thereby avoids attaching to them any one meaning to the exclusion of others. He leaves the matter open, points out what is incomplete and leaves the reader to make the synthesis.

[2] As Bouyer shows in his outstanding book *La Bible et l'Évangile* ("Lectio Divina" 8, 1951), whose subtitle "Du Dieu qui parle au Dieu fait homme" sums up the trend of this essay.

in this faith the word of God was always living and, as it were, incarnate by anticipation. And if this faith of the fathers pointed from the outset to the messiah, it was nevertheless firmly rooted in its constantly renewed origin, in Abraham, Moses, David and the prophets. Christ, both as man and as the son of God, fulfilled the religion of the people in absolute fidelity to it. This faith of Abraham's as the type of all faith, the faith of Sinai with its assent to the living law as the sign of the promise and the ever-present guidance of yahweh, the faith of Amos and Isaiah in the rights of the poor, the peaceable and the persecuted, the faith of Jeremias and Job, this certainly was the "faith" of Christ, the head and author of our faith, who brings it to fulfillment as ἀεχηγὸς παὶ τελειοτὴς τῆς ηίστέως (Heb 12:2). His vision of the father does not in anyway prevent his fulfilling the human and basic outlook of all the true servants of yahweh. How else could the believers in their faith follow Christ? For this faith did not begin with him, nor was he its sole object. It was not merely faith in him but faith together with him, faith in the full biblical sense, that is, in God, the God of Abraham, Isaac and Jacob, who now has revealed himself as God and father of the word, who is his son. The propensity of Christianity to impute to the chosen people an enormity of guilt is to be attributed to its inadequate understanding of the unity of all the truths vouched for in the bible. The categories of platonism (material and spiritual sense, type and antitype, analogy and anagogy) do not suffice to encompass this unique living unity. The adolescent (in this instance the early christian community) thinks he has to turn his back on his childhood and look solely to the future, but the mature

100

man turns his gaze backward to it. With all its faults the chosen people strove to make its decision for God on our behalf, strove and suffered through the centuries down to the time of Christ—and how much since—for us. We are engrafted in the sacred stem, in a close spiritual unity of life such as is to be found nowhere else in the world, even though the center of this unity is now revealed in Christ.

The dialectical unity between the two opposing poles of love and jealousy, as described by Paul in Rom 9–11, is also the mystery of the redemption of all mankind in Abraham, the father of all believers. At the time when this truth was first proclaimed there was no scripture, tradition, dogma, liturgy, law, priesthood or hierarchy. All this came later, the outcome of the decisive assent of naked man to naked God, who "reputed it to him unto justice." This nakedness of man before God was climaxed on the cross, where the opposition between Jew and pagan, between tradition and nontradition, was finally concluded and superseded (Eph 2:11f), but only in an eschatological setting.[1]

There are always further stages on the way to fulfillment. The entrance on the promised land after forty years in the desert was a first fulfillment, but no less so were the exile and scattering of the people, and likewise the son going about on earth, the church in its pilgrimage through the desert of the centuries (Ap 12:14), and each individual believer walking in hope. The whole of scripture is under way, always starting out afresh, wandering through the desert, from image to truth, from promise to fulfillment,

[1] See "The Sion Letters" in *The Bridge,* vol 1, New York 1956; also the report on the judeo-christian week in Berlin in the June 1957 *Herder-Korrespondenz;* and finally my own book on Buber, *Martin Buber and Christianity,* New York 1962.

101

from word to flesh, but also from the death of the body to the life of the spirit, moving from the fleshly present (through absence in death and ascension) to the eschatological present: the whole of this truth is a continuous forward striving ("diastasis"); it is the truth of the "cor inquietum," of hope and love for what is absent. It is into *this* human experience that the divine truth comes to embed itself. This delicate network of temporal relationships is strong enough to hold the absolute truth, which is itself a truth of eternal relations in an eternal life.

Revelation never falls directly from heaven to make supramundane mysteries known to men. God speaks to man from within the world, taking man's own experiences as a starting point, entering so intimately into his creature that the divine kenosis, to be fulfilled later in the incarnation, already has its beginning in the word of the old testament.

2

The next question concerns the mode of commuication devised to correspond to human experience. How does man speak to man? Let us try, first, to describe the essence of the matter in outline.

Human speech is the free manifestation of one's inner personality to others in significant sounds. It comprises three elements:

1) Self-possession on the part of the spiritual person, who is present to himself and so knows his own *truth*. Therefore his utterance is not just a confused sound, an incoherent effort to express an obscure inwardness, but an

102

exact, precise emission. This is precisely what characterizes the utterances of yahweh in contrast with the mystical babblings and impotent speechlessness at the higher reaches of other religions. "I am the lord that speak justice, that declare right things" (Is 45:19).

2) Possession of one's own truth means perfect *freedom*. Consequently the word chosen by the free man to express himself is not determined of necessity. Human speech, with all its bondage to imagery, must rest basically on a free choice of expression. The risen Christ had become, even in his bodily aspect, spiritual, that is to say, free. No longer was he known in a natural, passive fashion but rather gave himself to be known from out himself at any time of his choosing. Herein was the fulfillment of the verbum caro, for now human nature in its entirety was at the word's service to be its expression.

3) In the truth and freedom that follows on self-possession the personal spirit is the *universal* and *necessary* element, which means that from the outset it goes beyond subjectivity and reaches out to other persons (in principle, every other person), its existence always implying a relationship to them. It means communion and mutual intercourse from the very beginning. Speech therefore is no mere epiphenomenon of man but an integral part of his very being; and the most recent philosophies, those that set out directly from the phenomenon of speech, are the philosophies going to the heart of the matter. According to them the verbum mentis that has its source in inmost being, and the love that causes and accompanies it, do not turn the person in on himself (as a superficial interpretation of Augustine's imago trinitatis might lead one to think), but rather reveal

103

the mystery of being through the mutuality of knowledge in love. The word of man reveals, if it is true, the very constituents of his being. It is a participation, given from the outset, in being ever irradiated by the Spirit, and so also in the word ever uttered in the heart of being by eternal love. In this word everything was made, everything subsists; and everything was made with it in view. For human nature (which bears within itself an unfathomable promise) was destined from the first to find its fulfillment in the free revelation and grace of the eternal word.

But truth, freedom and love are not sufficient to characterize speech as specifically human. It is only human when it transcends itself in two directions, toward its origin in the past and toward its goal in the future.

1) The free spiritual speech of man emerges from the deep-lying interconnection of all parts of nature, revealed for the first time by modern biology and paleontology, which makes man the summit of the whole material and organic creation and its mouthpiece before God. Man as spirit dwells in being in its totality, and likewise through his body he dwells in the whole of nature, and can never detach himself from it. He speaks a corporeal, organic language, one of natural sounds and gestures. Hence there comes about the marvelous and multifarious interplay of nature and spirit in our speech, the gradual transition from natural images to half-emancipated symbols and then to freely chosen signs. These stages of transition from the speech of the whole body (as in the dance) to that of the tongue and distinct syllables, from physiognomy to abstract logic and grammar, all this wealth of resources gives us some idea of what sort of being man is, a being of inexhaustible

104

potentialities. Nor must we forget what modern biology tells us of the speech of animals, the unsuspected exactness of their means of communication with one another, the beginnings of abstraction and the systematization of their expression in the play of gesture, their often highly complex rituals so marvelously approximating to the sign language of primitive man. It is only in our technological age that the confidential relationship between man and nature that bore him has in great part been shattered. The romantics sought to recover this dimension of speech when it was almost extinct; but the attempt came too late. Nonetheless man remains, whether he likes it or not, a part of nature, and he will never wholly free himself from the sphere of natural signs. Mathematical logic will never be a human logic or even its substitute.

In this connection we might mention the sacraments and the liturgy. Both correspond with man as a part of nature and neither is so much the effect of a free, arbitrary ordinance on the part of God as of an accommodation of divine revelation to the actual laws of creation. Guardini brings out well the intimate relationship between the liturgy and the performance of sacred drama as a function shared both by individuals and all peoples.[1] We now know that Christ did not introduce any new sacramental signs. He took over baptism from John, the meal of bread and wine from the contemporary assemblies of the devout; and confession, required by the Baptist, is a general human practice to be found in all religions and even in buddhist monasteries. Anointing with oil and imposition of hands were part of a

[1] *Church and the Catholic, and the Spirit of the Liturgy,* New York 1940.

105

jewish ritual in which the liturgy of the mass was in great part foreshadowed.

2) Now for the second way in which human speech transcends itself, as regards its end. Speech is not its own fulfillment; it is related to life, it is creative and operative. It is itself a beginning of action, and goes beyond itself in its involvement with life and its activities. The time comes when speaking is not enough, when the witness of the whole person is imperative, as in married love, in politics, in the apostolate, in martyrdom. On the human plane truth does not exist without the virtue of truthfulness, which alone shows whether the true, righteous word has measured up to being itself and has not in some way fallen short. Thus in the bible the whole range of truth (veritas, veracitas, fidelitas) is covered by the one word emeth. God himself, no less than man, has bound himself by his word. God's word as well as man's looks toward what exists. In contrast with dumb idols incapable of a true word because they possess no fidelity and no reality, it bears within itself the witness and power of the living God. And after having long exercised its prophetic office the word passes into a new stage, that of the eucharist and the passion. This is what John means by "unto the end" (eis télos). What the spoken word could not do—it only provoked increasing resistance—was done by the sacrificed word slowly dissolving in the words of the cross and, finally, fading away in the tremendous, inarticulate death cry which sums up all —the spoken and the unspoken and the inexpressible—that God had to communicate to us. Of speaking there might be no end ("the world would not be able to contain the books"), but death puts the full stop. But even of action

106

there might be no end; suffering and death is man's last word, in which he gathers up his whole being before the father. It is his testament, the witness and final sealing of his life. His death makes of his lifetime and his word the unity God willed in his grace, which he chose as the highest expression of his own divine unity, the unity of his revelation and of his trinity of persons.

Just as we spoke, in connection with the first transcendence of the word and its involvement with nature and its organic activities, of the sacraments and the liturgy so here also must we speak of them in connection with its second mode of transcendence. For in the sacraments and the liturgy the word of Christ becomes act; his truth, now made evident to us and assured, becomes active and triumphant in us. This second transcendence is attained only in complete self-surrender. There is no christian liturgy without the sacrifice of the cross; in fact we might say that the two are one and the same.

Therefore man speaks as a free, spiritual person, as one who knows truth; he expresses both nature and himself in his concrete existence. It is this speech that God has chosen as his means of revelation. This means that revelation presupposes in the created order a fundamental analogy of being; but analogy is described (according to the Fourth Lateran Council) as "in tanta similitudine major dissimilitudo." For as we have shown the free speech of man presupposes a speech of nature devoid of freedom, since man is a corporeal and organic being. But between God and the world there is no necessary bond of union; creation, revelation, redemption are all absolutely free decisions of God. Yet there is a real analogy governing this sphere. Man's spiritual speech presupposes the speech of nature, and the speech of revelation presupposes for its part the speech of God's creation, in fact this analogy of being, and in consequence a natural knowledge of God, or expressed in religious terms a natural, concrete sense of the creature for the being from which it proceeds, a cognitio per contactum (Thomas), which persists through each individual existence and the whole historical course of peoples and cultures. The analogy goes even further; for as the free word of the spirit represents, in relation to the speech of nature (the speech of animals or infants for example), a completely new stage, so also does the free speech of God when he reveals himself by intervening in human history. He comes as the subject who is sovereign, teaching, acting, choosing and rejecting, judging and giving grace, according to laws known to him alone and not derivable from the existing laws of existence or of history. And yet the existence of such freedom of utterance is experienced by man before divine revelation makes use of it. It is precisely this experience, in which human freedom, rising superior to nature, attains speech that God appropriates in order to show man that he is his lord and that he acts in perfect freedom.

From these basic premises we draw three conclusions.
1) God speaks his word within man. Not only what man utters but all that he is becomes God's organ of communication. What man is and can be is only revealed in its fullness when God makes of him his alphabet, his sounding board and sense organ. God in his freedom decided to become man, chose his creature's mode of expression in order

to reveal the hidden things of his divinity, and resolved to pour out the abyss of his riches into that other abyss of emptiness and indigence, in order to find his glory in the shame of the cross and in the descent to hell. Once he decided to do all this (and he did so before he made the world, the creation being the first step on the way), then from the very beginning his word regarded man's whole existence and experience as an aspect of the mode of expression. Moreover in revelation man found God central to man. The veil of secondary causes is not torn away; on the contrary the more God reveals himself the more deeply does he conceal himself in men. The word that in the beginning seemed to sound from heaven, somewhat apart and self-contained, now hides itself in the body of Christ, in the sacraments, in the church's preaching, in the teaching of theologians, in the liturgical, administrative and hierachical activities of the church. But all this is always man's doing. He is called to encounter God and he comes to know him in living faith, through the mysterious touches and stirrings in the depths of his soul which make him aware of God's presence and action. But we cannot come to the father otherwise than in the humanity of his son, and only in the mystical body of Christ have we a part in the Spirit of both. To love God we must love our neighbor, and in the humility of brotherly love we will come to know him who is eternal. Yet if man is the utterance of God he is never God himself; and to know God he must both realize and deny himself. He is what God says but never the one who says. To reveal God he must conceal, forget, extinguish himself. He will only succeed in this when he gives up all his experiences and situations, all his powers

109

and faculties, for God to use, as the compositor uses the
letters lying before him.

2) The particular word of God that we call the biblical
revelation, and which is always the center of the divine
utterance, passes necessarily beyond itself into a total human word, by referring back to the creation and its word
and forward to the judgment on the world and the resurrection of the whole of history in God. From Christ as the
center of history there falls the light that illumines its beginning and end, illumines so-called natural religion[1] and
eschatology. The religion of the patriarchs derives in part
from the religion of Canaan; Abraham we see paying homage to Melchisedech, David's ancestor in Salem, later to be
elevated to become the type of Christ. In the bible we have
the pre-abrahamic saints, Abel and Enoch, brought to light
by the sacred writers, together with the bright constella-
tion Noah, Daniel and Job mentioned by Ezechiel. The later
God of Israel called yahweh is found under strange and perhaps confused names, those of the gods of Canaan, of the
gods of mountain and storm, all those divine forces which,
no doubt, originally represented the elohim, already the God
of the revelation to come. In the name and authoritative
commission of the God of Israel the sacred writers make
this identification, and assume the responsibility for it.
Gradually the messianic vision broadens out the jewish
religion until it envisages the whole universe, the salvation
of all peoples through the mediation of Israel. And cor-
respondingly theological reflection sets out a universal his-

[1] Or more precisely the religion deriving from the actual creation,
from the stirrings of the grace originally given and from the workings
of a secret hope, both natural and supernatural.

110

tory of creation and, what is even more astonishing, anticipates the covenant with Abraham by a divine covenant with Noah, a covenant which God established expressly with the whole of mankind, with all flesh, in fact "with every living thing" and "for perpetual generations;" further, the sign of this eternal reconciliation between God and the world was one taken from nature. The priests of Israel put the question: whence comes the marvelous stability of the cosmic order in face of the grave sinfulness of the human race? And the answer given is that the grace of God, who revealed himself to Israel, embraces the whole earth and all the generations of man along with their idols and perverted religions.

3) Since the word of God is directed to the whole of mankind as the offspring of God, nothing human is alien to it. Every human situation can be brought to bear, every kind of contact between two persons, man and wife, father and son, mother and child, king and people, priest and layman, prophet and temple, personal and ritual religion, political and religious communities, love, hatred, jealousy, mercy, fidelity, self-sacrifice to the point of the vows which bind a man for ever, to the point of martyrdom whereby he renounces his own life.

And there is something else of equal moment. The word of God takes hold of the people of Israel in its historical place as bound up with a general evolution, not only in its political situation between the great powers to the east of it, not only in its cultural dependence on the Phoenicians (whose architects built the temple, whose poets influenced the form of a number of the psalms), but on the deeper level of philosophy of life, wisdom, metaphysics and reli-

111

gion. All these progress, especially in the ancient world, according to a kind of unitary law governing the entire development of human nature and the formation of a consciousness of mankind as a whole. We see the different human dimensions developing one after the other, and placing themselves at the free disposition of God's word. Each stage of development *can* (should God wish to make use of it) become the necessary condition for a new stage of revelation. It is due to this connection of Israel's historical process with that of mankind that, in a certain sense, the laws of world history arrange themselves in subordination to those of the history of revelation.[1]

The fact is that since God wills to use human speech the revelation of the one true God waits until a kind of syncre-

---

[1] Since God himself chooses, in sovereign freedom, the means and material conditions for his revelation our theory can satisfy the most stringent requirements of the analogia fidei, as put forward by Karl Barth. It does so in that the same God, as creator, prepares beforehand the elements in human history that he wills to make use of as revealer. The space between the general history of culture and the history of revelation is subject to the law of the analogia entis (between creation and God), which certainly does not invalidate our first consideration.

All this has been constantly upheld in the apologetics of the fathers, who laid down the general guidelines, and in the textbooks; for instance the treatment of Christ's sacrifice is introduced by wide-ranging reflections on the idea of sacrifice common to all peoples (ritual sacrifice, expiatory sacrifice, inner sacrifice, etc.). Now however the latest biblical discoveries permit us to discern within the bible itself the actual historical connection of "natural religion" (with all its deformations due to sin, and so sharply censured by the word of God) and "supernatural religion." In virtue of this development we can now go beyond the abstract juxtaposition of the traditional treatises "de religione in genere" and "de revelatione supernaturali."

It is also clear that our view by no means conduces to total evolutionism or religious liberalism of any kind since it is a logical application of the law of God's incarnation in man, who has to be taken in his totality.

tistic monotheism has been attained by Egypt and Babylon
for it to be understood at all worthily and as it should be.
It presupposes the system of the Amphyctyonians (the
union of the twelve tribes) already reached. The idea of a
God leading the people must have gained a certain universal currency, must have been present in a general way
to men's minds for it to be superseded by that of yahweh
who, when introduced in medio deorum, reduces every
other divinity to nothing. The concept of the anointed king
as a visible image of the invisible God, that of a sacred
polity underlying the secular, the image of the wise man, of
the prophet with his special gifts, of the mediator of salvation, of the messiah, of the seer of what transcends the
visible world, a wisdom literature orientated to the end of
of time—all these ideas are found far beyond the boundaries
of Israel. It is not just a matter of literary forms[1] that God
"applies" in his revelation or adopts for his purposes. What
he does is to associate himself in the most intimate fashion
with each new form of human experience.

While secular history is not to be confused with sacred
history, it must nevertheless be admitted that today we see
what the fathers called the praeparatio evangelica, the logos
spermatikos and its development, in an entirely new, much
more positive light. But the order they assumed is now inverted. It is not Plato who was dependent on Moses but

[1] It would be an evasion of the problem to see it solely in literary
terms and to speak of literary forms as if there were only an external
relationship between God's word and its human expression, and that
God could have used equally well any other appropriate form. One
might then say that God could just as well have been incarnated in
Paul or Augustine as in Christ. It would be overlooking the essential
truth that God does not take man's word out of his mouth and put it
into his own, but rather makes the whole man the word of God.

113

Moses on "Plato," that is to say, on the egyptian view of the world and egyptian wisdom. This is expressly stated in scripture (Acts 7:22). In consequence, even if the general evolution of mankind is reflected in the bible, we cannot draw from it any kind of systematic theology of world history or of the history of culture. All we can conclude is that the development of man's awareness of the unity of the human race, which we call "progress," is intimately connected with revelation.[1]

[1] We can no longer speak of various independent species of progress in universal history. The more we understand the implication of human reflection—meditation on the past, prayer, suffering for and through God—in the course of the sacred history of both the old and new testaments, of the synagogue and the church, the more we perceive a convergence (never an identity) of "natural" and "supernatural" progress. There are not two but three modalities of progress: that of revelation (completed with the death of the last apostle), that of the development of doctrine (or the church's reflection on revelation), and that of secular history. The fact that a certain "supernatural progress" continues in the new testament serves to answer a possible objection, namely that the evolution of man (assuming there is one) in the two millennia before Christ is so slight in comparison with that of the universe that its effect in sacred history can tell us nothing either about the meaning of evolution as a whole or about the relations of the forms of progress. But it must be noted that the ideas here put forward permit certain inner analogies to be drawn, analogies that can on no account be transposed into identities. On the one hand there is an inner analogy between the progress of revelation and that of doctrine, and this in two respects: 1) in both cases the obedience and religious reflection of the believer *can* impel a new intervention of the Spirit of God (as is clearly evidenced in the epoch of the wise men of Israel and in Judaism, as also in the time of the prophets); 2) in both cases however it is ultimately this Spirit of God who guides history and its developments, and this in perfect freedom. On the other hand there is an equally inner analogy (although of instrumental causality) between "supernatural" and "natural" progress since, in both cases, progress means growth in inwardness and universality, and thus the capacity to control a wider range of data. The decisive progress of the old testament consists in the advance from tribal to national consciousness and finally, through

114

There is one more conclusion to be drawn, and we need not avoid it since it was drawn long ago by the church fathers. It is that the new stage of consciousness reached by western man—the discovery of being (and so of abstract and necessary ideas, the universalism of reason) by the Greeks—seems to be one of the final "prerequisites" of man if the incarnation is to take place. Without it the necessary basis for the preaching of a gospel to the whole of mankind would be lacking, or at least not present in a way intelligible to us and appropriate to our mentality. Not only would the corresponding means of expression be lacking but even the definite human experiences and categories of thought necessary for understanding the significance of Christ as bearing upon the whole universe of being would be absent. Here too we see the synthetic action of revelation; the unity realized by Christ is prepared beforehand and, in this preparation, anticipated. If the synthesis between judaism and hellenism was already achieved at Christ's coming it was surely because the peace brought in his body between two parts of mankind (Eph 2:16) should not be established only outside and beyond history, and because

---

the exile, to a universal consciousness which gave the thinkers of Israel some intimation that the salvation of all peoples was involved in sacred history. The new testament reflects a parallel advance of the universalistic idea in Paul's and John's development of the synoptics; and thus the progress of doctrine consists in a constantly deepening insight that results from an ever more comprehensive vision. Only we must not forget the operation, in all three domains, of the law by which some loss is suffered with the advance of time, a law Augustine and Gregory the Great were so conscious of. In the last analysis there are not two lines of progress because there are not two universalisms existing side by side, for the human (abstract) universal of the natural order is always subordinate to the (concrete) universal of Christ, in whom all things are brought together into unity.

115

christian faith should find already present in the world the elements conducive to an understanding of this mystery.

Human wisdom, however much God may use it in his revelation, is never dispensed from the obligation of dying unto itself. The wisdom of this world must avow itself to be foolishness in order to become the wisdom of God. Even in its literary form as given by the human writer the word of the bible is an integral part of the word that judges and gives grace. The books of Job, Ecclesiastes and the Proverbs may be composed after the manner of the egyptian and accadish books of wisdom, but the complaints of the man in his abandonment or his resignation in face of the transience of this life take on a quite different coloring by the mere fact of being incorporated into scripture, not to speak of the inner transformation they undergo. Various stages of progress are recorded in the course of sacred history, only to be abandoned. Consider the wandering of Elias, which took him back over the footsteps of Moses, though in the reverse direction. He left the promised land to go into the desert, and once again we see the terrifying mountain, once again the manifestation of the holy one in storm, earthquake and fire. But the times have advanced; God is no longer in these things but in the pneuma, in the gentle wind of the spirit.

There is a stage when the word adapts itself to the level of a culture and the stage when it transcends it. But this adaptation involves no compromise; God always reveals himself as the free, the absolute subject. Man must always make a detour to find God, make a confession, and this goes against the grain; God does not lie at the terminus of man's desires and ideals, nor is he to be reached through

116

human asceticism and mysticism—even when carried to their highest point. All human experiences must serve God; but he is not committed to any, not does he take over any without transforming them in his purifying flame. His word is freedom, is power. His word suffices to impel the resisting, obstinate, unfaithful Israel, in a matter of centuries, through all the humiliations, from the primitive tribal consciousness of the nomads right up to the threshold of the gospel. And how extraordinary to find the song of God's servant in the old testament! All this is due solely to the power of the living word, working like leaven from within. Into this resistant material comes the revelation, growing in depth, not only of the majesty of the transcendent God, surpassing all the immanent gods, but also of the humility, the vulnerability of the divine love, the concern of the divine heart which reveals itself in the humiliated human heart. Blessed are the poor, for God in all his riches is eternal "poverty." Blessed are the humble, for God in his majesty is the eternally "humble." God himself in his eternal ascent—ascendit Deus—is eternal abasement, eternal descent—quia et descendit primum. In Job deserted by all, in Jeremias, in the captives of Babylon, in the poor of yahweh crying to heaven and receiving no answer, in all these types of dereliction we see a revelation of the divine heart in its abandonment. And after the great light of the religion of the word and of the revelation of the true God, his being and nature, it is still, once again, what man knew from the beginning, and what the Areopagite was to recall to the minds of christians: God is the absolute mystery whom we can but adore.

God reveals himself in man in order to bring him to

117

adore what no eye has seen. God sends his son to express the father in human guise. We hear the father in his human echo; in a human obedience to death we come to experience who it is that commands it; *in the answer we have the word.* The son as man, at the summit of the cosmos, executes before the father the ecclesiastic, the cosmic liturgy. In him are joined word and liturgy.

3

Of him, of Jesus Christ, we have still to treat. In him alone but through him for all men the word of God is hypostatically one with man. In him human existence in time comes, as we saw in the first part, to a parity with the truth. Between the divine and human natures of Christ nothing is discordant; what God wills to say about himself is fully and precisely stated in this utterance, this man. Consummatum est. It is not beyond our reach or understanding, it has attained its end. Homo capax Dei. Human speech, as we saw in the second part, contains in itself the whole of nature and the whole moral life, the entire history of man; and here its scope extends to the eternal word of the father, here every ideal is realized, so that anyone who builds on this ground bases his ideal on a reality. The plenitude has been reached, the end of history is present, all the temporal dimensions have been fulfilled. All this happens in a simple human life with nothing exceptional about it save an ardent love for the father and for men, a life of work and teaching, ending in poverty and disgrace. Its glorification after death was accredited by only a few witnesses; for there was

118

nothing here which world history could take cognizance of: only a man, the son of man.

Nevertheless in Jesus, a man unique and aware of his uniqueness, the word of God reached men. God's word is no longer an abstract law, it is this man. Everything God had to say or give to the world has found a place in him. The whole objective spirit of religion, of law, of ritual is identical with the subjective spirit of this particular man, a man like us. It is the religion of freedom. When this man gives God his all, obeys him to death, he obeys but himself, his love as son for the father. With him it is no longer any question of heteronomy or of autonomy; the "heteros," the father, is also "tò autón," the same concrete nature. He who believes in the son is free, for he has attained to the true, absolute humanism.

The word of God that is heard in our liturgies reaches far beyond the sphere of the church. It is the lord of secular history, of the office and factory, of science and politics. All this it contains within itself, and this is but a small part of the treasures of wisdom and knowledge hidden therein. The liturgy of the church pays him homage, in knowledge and love, whereas the world does not know its master, and seeks to crucify him anew. But the liturgy, now prostrate before him, must in the end raise itself up and seek to realize in the secular sphere what it preaches and promises in the spiritual.

Revelation and the Beautiful

The *and* of the title should startle the reader, or at least give him a feeling of profound unease. It is a word that conjoins two spheres that have generally been held quite disparate, particularly by writers of a generation not far removed from our own. We recall how Kierkegaard, at an audience with the queen, was congratulated by her on his incomparable work *Either* and *Or,* an incident that serves to emphasize unwittingly the sad omission of any possible conjunction between the two concepts of the title, concepts which, since Kierkegaard's eruption into the protestant and catholic thought of our century, have dominated christian ideology. The first thing that a serious student of that time had to observe was the separation of the esthetic and ethical spheres, particularly where a christian ethic or religion was concerned. Thus at a single stroke the false associations and identifications of a century and more were thrown over. But the esthetic had a strange power of attraction. When put aside it does not rest until as myth, eros, framework of thought or hegelian kingdom of ideas it comes finally to dominate all the rest, and to incorporate christianity as a way to itself or as an intermediary or as a last stage in the ascent. Thus, to vindicate the place christianity claims for itself, the esthetic must be summarily dismissed (by omitting the and), since relegating it to a subordinate role is not sufficient.

Kierkegaard's austere position would not have met such general acceptance had it not been in conformity with a number of ideas then in the air and brought by him into the light of day. Doubtless esthetics is a young science insofar as the idea of the beautiful, previously embedded in that of the true and the good, was only liberated from the latter to any degree toward the close of the enlightenment —though the process began with the renaissance—and completely so in the period of German idealism. This was not just a question of method but of a whole philosophy; and in a certain respect the epoch of classicism and romanticism, of Schleiermacher, Schelling, Hegel and Schopenhauer was one of "estheticism." This aspect of the age implies no evaluation, but it does mean that the idea of the beautiful takes on a certain independence of the two cognate ideas from which it had been hitherto inseparable. It is this divorce from its background which is perilous, the beginning of an "estheticization" of the beautiful. Can the idea of the beautiful remain always the same in a period of historicism which sets itself above the form taken by beauty in the art of all peoples and times, an historicism arranging the various manifestations of art in a systematic and chronological order and so inaugurating a new way of contemplating it? And can the traditional idea of beauty subsist at all and be subsumed with the new under a common concept in an epoch of materialism and psychoanalysis, in the twentieth century when art is mainly concerned with proclaiming purely material relationships of space, surfaces and bodies and (what comes to the same thing) with representing the structural elements of the unconscious mind? The critical state we have reached may be summed up by noting that whereas previously there was a generally accepted metaphysics establishing a living bond between the immanent sciences and the transcendent christian revelation, it has now become quite unreal and ineffectual and has been abandoned in favor of the immanence of the sciences. If this is so then Kierkegaard's *Either-Or* is not just a piece of warped and stunted protestant Weltanschauung but also a clear expression of the contemporary situation, which (according to Hegel, but not Kierkegaard) always has reason on its side, and which the man of reason, even when he is a christian, must take into account. Thus there came into existence a number of catholic "kierkegaardians," just as we now have catholic "picassoists." The two are closely connected. The "daimonia" esthetic which Kierkegaard propounded in his much admired but incredibly false analysis of Mozart is present also in his *Esthetic Stage,* which likewise involves an antireligious "cynicism," as well as the intrinsic necessity for the dialectical, existential form in which it is finally contained. The one thing certainly lacking in this theory of daimonia (as also in Goethe's "grotesque") is an understanding of what the daimon meant to Plato.

Martin Deutinger was the last of the catholic thinkers[1] in the period 1840–1860 to consider the two spheres as inseparably joined. Because of this view he was summarily

---

[1] There were of course subsequent attempts in the same direction, among which the curious work of G. M. Dursch deserves mention: *Der Symbolische Charakter der christlichen Religion und Kunst* 1860, also Jungmann's esthetic (first edition 1865, second with many changes 1884), not to mention Dyroff's esthetic which appeared in a limited edition.

assigned to the category of the romantics, whose ideology is outdated, along with the protestant successors of the idealists who, more logical and subtle than the great masters, occupied themselves with the concordance of beauty and revelation: Christian Weisse, Immanuel Hermann von Fichte, Herman Ulrici, Conrad Hermann and the encyclopedic Moritz Carrière. For us (who do not know them any longer) they are at best communicators of the ideas of others, and it is impossible to say who among them might have continued their line of thought. At any rate it is hard to imagine how it could have influenced a theology no longer informed by a living philosophy, for in recent theology all that is presupposed and contained in philosophy is no more than an outline, a propaedeutic for the use of seminarians, not the deep reflections of the great scholastics —and such an outline has no room for esthetics. However, rather than dwell on the justifiable complaint that recent dogmatic mores are lacking in any real feeling for beauty (all too often in their style), it is more important to concentrate on the far greater danger menacing speculative theology, namely the kind of paralysis induced by a biblical criticism which dominates the whole field, and claims to have a monopoly of scientific precision in the modern sense. It is quite impossible to see how this could have any point of contact with esthetics. Yet this is also part of the spirit of the age, and we would be guilty of ingratitude did we not acknowledge how much that was wrongfully neglected in the past is here powerfully reinstated, how much that is essential for a future theology is here made available. The spirit of our age then has its advantages, though it owes its driving force in part to a loss of the power of synthesis. Yet, after all, there cannot be any fruitful thinking in theology that does not start out from its essential center. A science is "exact" when its method exactly corresponds to its object; and one whose method of its very nature only relates to the partial aspect in current favor of the whole object can only with reserve be called exact. As regards the word of God there is no such thing as a purely human, purely historical and philological aspect in isolation from the divine and so from the dogmatic aspect. This is what is questionable about a procedure that prescinds from speculation or contemplation, questionable that is from the intuitive standpoint which, in virtue of its comprehensive range, keeps the fundamental framework of the object within its vision— something impossible, in the case of a sacred object, to a detached, remote standpoint. What has happened, in modern theology, to the "frui" of the fathers and the medievals?

How are we to recover, now, in the present day, after such a lapse of time, what has been lost? Merely refastening the thread where it broke in the time of Deutinger is out of the question. There is only one thing that might be successful: without breaking the tradition (as materialism and psychoanalysis fundamentally do) to seek out the basic elements in Kierkegaard's two spheres, the esthetic and the ethico-religious, and thereby to understand afresh how revelation and the idea of the beautiful came together originally in the christian tradition of the west.

1

The theological element in esthetics viewed historically

It has always seemed the greatest paradox in the history of esthetics that the founder of the science, Plato, was a declared enemy of the "esthetic;" from the *Ion* to the *Gorgias* and the two *Hippias,* from the *Republic* to the *Laws,* he inveighed incessantly against art and artists. What was the real significance of this stance, apart from certain incidental exaggerations uttered in the heat of controversy? The mystical world, as represented for the Greeks by Homer and Hesiod in particular, when no longer taken seriously, provided no basis either for individual life or that of the state. Formerly it could have been and in fact was the only possible basis. Politics, as the creative formation of the polis, religion as the magical and mythical bond between political life and the tutelary deity of the people, art as the visible seal of this covenant between heaven and earth (the noblest example being the egyptian bas-reliefs and paintings, where king and God stand face to face, or the divine bird inspiring the king covers his head with its wings), these three, so long as the myth was a living one, formed a perfect unity. It is possible therein to enshrine a certain tradition of "wisdom," as is proved by all the high cultures from Egypt to China, but the wisdom consists in the real, concrete sense of the integration of the three into a single whole, as against any kind of separation on abstract principles, which would be fatal.

126

By contrast, in Greece philosophy (together with skepticism of the indivisible myth) and the idea of the individual emerged simultaneously, but in such a way that the older mythological tradition, which offered such varied material, was put to a severe test. By the poets it was regarded as a kind of assumption, an "as if;" in the great tragedies its ambiguity could bring out the tragic alternation in human life between piety and despair. But this "esthetic" ground, according to Plato, provided no solid basis on which to build reality. Poets and painters make use of appearances but they do not attain reality. "Should the tragedians knock at the gates of the new state, saying: O strangers, may we go to your city or may we not, and shall we bring with us our poetry? How shall we rightly answer these divine men? I think our answer should be as follows: Best of strangers, we also, according to our ability, are tragic poets, and our tragedy is the best and noblest; for our whole state is an imitation of the best and noblest life, which we affirm to be the very truth of tragedy. Wherefore, o ye sons and scions of the softer Muses, first of all show your songs to the magistrates, and let them compare them with our own, and only if they find that yours contain the same principles or better, will we authorize you a choir for their performance; but, in the contrary case, dear friends, it will not be possible" (Plato, *Laws* VII, 817, a–d). The drama of reality, in which not fantasy but the requirements of being coincident with the good dictate the course of the play, must be performed. But what is the good, the divine being? Plato attempted to answer by pursuing two lines of thought. The first, leading by degrees from the manifold of beautiful things to the idea of the good and the beautiful, he described most engagingly

127

in the *Symposium* and the *Phaedrus,* where the enquiry was about the power and essence of eros, and where it was seen as a longing to attain the depths of the divine and absolute, made visible to the lover in the beautiful form of the beloved; a longing therefore which, without ceasing to embrace the concrete, can only love it in its relation to the infinite. The man who does not love knows nothing, but eros wills, by generating, to come to rest in the beloved. In surrender to the object as it is there is also a will to creation and formation—proceeding from love and not, as later with Aristotle, as technics and imitation (completion) of nature. It is here that Plato comes nearest to the christian metaphysic of the trinity, though he does not develop it, to the trinitarian "filius meus es tu."

But the theory of ideas failed its creator in the course of his argument. All that remained was the order established eternally in the actual cosmos, the harmony between natures and essences conceived as eternal numbers, of which the earthly city was to be the authentic reproduction. In both the *Philebos* and the *Symposium* the pleasure to be found in eros is relegated to a subordinate place: "Pleasure is not the first property, nor yet the second. The first is measure and that which contains it (metrion) and the fitting (kairion). . . . The second, consequently, concerns the conformable (symmetron) and the beautiful and the perfect and the corresponding (hikanon)" (*Phileb* 66a), in such wise however that the first and the second are not opposed as the perfect idea and its inadequate reproduction in time and space, but as the measure of the real divine world and the being which contains this measure, being determined in its nature by it and expressed by it. The subhuman world has no feeling for the structure of life through the divine numbers, for "rhythm and harmony;" but "to us are given the gods as our companions and as givers of the feeling for rhythm and harmony and joy in these." The ceremoniousness pervading both public and private life testifies (as in China) to the sacred nature of the cosmos (*Laws* II, 653e–654a). We can leave undecided whether this second solution is a reversion to the order of myth, as in fact is the case with the *Timaeus.* For us the important thing is that, in both ways, Plato can only erect his ethical doctrine on a basis of esthetics. Art driven out by the fork of philosophical seriousness returns on a plane even higher than philosophy, as the sacred art of right living in which the holiness of the divine order of the world finds its embodiment. The kalon and agathon is the vision of the holy itself (hieron) as "a mystery most blessed, shining in pure light" (*Phaedrus* 250), and in the second course of the argument, as the holiness of being, which is not elicited by the genius of the inspired artist or derived from him, but something originating as a gift from above and which must be handed down to the people as a living thing.

We have dwelled on this example because it is characteristic of something that constantly recurs. The great thinkers who at various times discussed the relationship between revelation and the beautiful always began by depreciating the latter, as if it had to be discarded in order to make way for the religious idea; only later, as a result of the cleavage, did the beautiful force its way back in the form of what was actually revealed. We will leave aside Plotinus, for whom the beautiful and the good merged effortlessly into a unity, and consider the case of Augustine. His conversion

129

was in the nature of a painful turning away from sensible beauty (as well as from that of the manichaean myth), and this privation was in some measure relieved by the teaching of Plotinus and the bittersweet substitution of a holy and spiritual beauty ("Beauty ever old and ever new, too late have I loved thee"). But later Plotinus was rejected and the latent esthetic of the early philosophical writings gave way to a second, obscure phase of conversion, to the cross, laid on him as a bishop, of routine pastoral cares with nothing esthetic about them. It is not on account of his *De Musica,* with its higher platonist occupations, that he is always regarded as the founder of christian esthetics, but rather through the measure and rhythm of his actual experience, moving to the very edge of profligacy but always caught back into the current of a pastoral office with its humiliations. The idea of the beautiful that he established streams from all the pores of his being. It is something far more profound than his too self-conscious style (when he cultivates it) whose beauty, in fact, is greatest when its content overwhelms it.

Among all the medieval thinkers Bonaventure applied himself most stringently to the theory of the beautiful. He might, simply as a thinker, well be counted among the platonist school were the strongly contrasted spirit of the early Franciscans not so pronounced in his thought and, still more, in his life. Both the "fioretti" and the theology, so attractive and beguiling in their care for harmony, expression and ecstasy, have their real source in Francis, who was always a stranger to the esthetic approach. However strongly the esthetic forced itself upon him and offered a framework for his life in its tremendous impact on the

130

times, Francis, despite his early activities as a troubadour, was essentially a very different kind of person. A later parallel is the relationship between Ignatius, a stranger in the world of art, and the impetus he gave to the baroque, an art form always conscious (at least in its best moments) that it was decorating something which no art can wholly grasp. Spanish art seems to have felt more keenly than any other that the most christian objects art depicts are precisely the least esthetic ones: the ignominy of the passion, the repugnant facts of martyrdom. Greco's art achieves its effect by a kind of renunciation, a reversion to earlier practice, inasmuch as the beauty of the human form he portrays is only attainable through the night of faith. We are not here concerned with the question whether it is technically possible for art to depict some event in which it sees itself repudiated. We merely note the fact that it cannot rise to the level of truth without having to experience a sense of repugnance.

The case of Kierkegaard, the most arresting and significant of modern times, can be explained as a special instance of this traditional law, at any rate so long as the *Either-Or* is not considered primarily as opposing esthetics to ethics (and so to the christian attitude) but rather as showing the impossibility of a purely esthetic attitude to life, and as proceeding in the second part to indicate directly and openly the possible synthesis. The two headings of this part reveal his intention: "The esthetic validity of marriage" and "The equilibrium between the esthetical and the ethical in the composition of personality;" and here we find to our astonishment a complete rejection of the supposed opposition between eros and agape, on the grounds

131

that there is in eros, in first, romantic love, a religious element demanding fidelity and constancy, and that marital
fidelity finds continuous support in the purity of this original
eros. "To me God has not become so supermundane that
he might not concern himself about the covenant he himself has established betwixt man and woman . . . And all the
beauty inherent in the pagan erotic has validity also in
Christianity, insofar as it can be combined with marriage"
(*Either-Or,* ed Lowrie, II,9). "Certainly, the God of the
Christians is Spirit, and Christianity is spirit, and discord
is posited between flesh and spirit; but 'the flesh' is not
sensuousness, it is selfishness, and, in this sense, even the
intellectual which you call 'spiritual' may be sensual; for
example, if a man takes in vain his intellectual gifts, he is
carnal. And I know well that, for Christians, it was not
necessary that Christ should be of an earthly beauty . . .
But it by no means follows from all this that the sensuous
is abolished by Christianity. First love has in it the factor
of beauty, and the joy and fullness which is found in the
sensuous when it is innocent can well be admitted into
Christianity" (42). "Be amazed at the harmonious accord
of these three spheres. It is the same thing, except that it is
expressed esthetically, religiously and ethically" (50). The
esthetic implies a provisional choice, but to cling to it would
be a refusal of choice. Choosing on the other hand (which
is what the ethical is) implies bringing into the inner sphere
what the esthetic shows outwardly as a mood. Here Kierkegaard is at one with Blondel, who takes the "esthetic" as
an attitude of life, as the rejected starting point of the philosophy which is centered on freely choosing God and
thereby gaining all, even all beauty. But is this all? Or has

132

beauty, for Kierkegaard, a lingering taste of what is for him unattainable, forbidden, since he is the one sacrificed, the one who renounces eros for the sake of God, or perhaps out of spleen or melancholy? Here the lines become entangled; and yet it is the extreme stress of his later years, in the form of martyrdom for the truth—which is, despite all, the expression of a purity—which gives even to the disorderly notes of the *Journals* the inimitable beauty of a mission fulfilled.

The last image: John of the Cross and Teresa. John, by profession a picture engraver, chooses the way of the "nothing and all," of entering and passing through the night and nakedness of faith. Yet it is by this means that he came to be Spain's greatest poet, for it was the experience he underwent which gave him the words no imitator, whatever his genius, could have found. The slight sketch of a vision of the cross shows, as do the poems, the complete elimination of esthetic vision and artistic technique in his mysticism. The same is true of Teresa, and Lacordaire's "There are not two kinds of love" is never more applicable than here. We might argue that there is something ambiguous in Bernini's statue of Teresa but this would simply be due to our inability to grasp in its entirety the sublime, paradisal nature of the perfectly pure eros; the Canticle of Canticles may be seen in the same light.

2

The theological element in esthetics viewed factually

It might be supposed from this title that the only true beauty is of a religious order, and that the shock which induces us to turn aside from the seeming beauty of the world is precisely some glimpse of the only true beauty. This then is the beauty that christian art, insofar as it is genuine, wishes to serve; this is the sun on which it attempts to gaze, and since it can not do so directly it perseveres reverently in its effort to make this beauty visible by means of those to whom grace has accorded this vision.

One may agree with this idea of a religious esthetic, but only if it is completed by accepting all the concrete kinds of beauty immanent in the world. These are of an almost inexhaustible variety and their combinations yield ever new variations, like the notes of a great organ. Their very richness is a proof of the transcendental origin of the beautiful, but only when the impact from above is truly felt. The form of the object may convey this impact, may even contain it as a special grace. Whether in fact this is transmitted to the receiver depends on the occasion, whether he has eyes, ears or heart for it, whether his hour has come, whether he is open and receptive to the beauty in question, whether the times are propitious for the manifestation of the beauty in things (not to be exposed in museums to the gaping crowds like captured beasts).

The beauty inherent in things is susceptible of degrees

134

from the lower to the higher, from the purely material and functional to the organic and sensible, and so from that of symmetry, proportion and harmony to that shown in vital tension and power, in the alternation of disclosure and concealment, in all the forms of interaction both inside and outside the erotic with its beguiling qualities. It includes all that in nature and in the human sphere serves to deck out the bare existence, whatever is agreeable, adornment, clothing, all the apparatus created to serve the purposes of society, its customs, distractions and prevailing modes of living. And everywhere there should be a correspondence between object and subject: the external harmony must correspond to a subjective need and both give rise to a new harmony of a higher order; subjectivity, with its feeling and imagination, must free itself in an objective work, in which it rediscovers itself, in the course of which (as in the fables of Novalis) there may be as much self-discovery as experience of another. Tension, disguise, transformation together constitute the drama, and it is not lacking in an element of cruelty, inevitably so, for man is a part of nature. Man's need and impulse to play and to shape things combine to produce the things of everyday life—a house, curtains, chairs, bed. The occasions for these are countless, and so also are the occasions for all the various forms of the beautiful which lie at his disposal. And since the beautiful comprises both tension and its release, and reconciliation of opposites by their interaction, it extends beyond its own domain and necessarily postulates its own opposite as a foil. The sublime has to be set off by the base, the noble by the comic and grotesque, even by the ugly and the horrible, so that the beautiful may have its due place in the whole,

135

and that a heightened value may accrue from its presence.

Yet all that the history of art and culture, archeology and sociology are mainly concerned with would be inadequate were it not polarized through the experience of the whole mystery of being and the origin of things, mysterium tremendum et fascinosum. It is this which has always been the unique real occasion of the great religious or "mythological" art of all peoples. It is from man's indigence and sense of power simultaneously, from his act of surrender and adjuration, that he comes to represent that tremendous reality which intervenes, in masterful fashion, in the great moments of the life both of peoples and of individuals. "For the beautiful is nothing else than the onset of the terrible, which we only just endure, and we admire it, because it calmly disdains to destroy us" (Rilke). *This* beauty has its own proper historical moment, a time when the primitive, simple terror of the numinous begins to weaken, when the stage of philosophical speculation about "the divine," secure and disenchanted, has not yet been reached—the stage when the beautiful is domesticated and in fact attained to its highest expression (as in periclean Athens), though it owes this ability to an earlier stage of development. Between the two periods mythology has its greatest scope when the revelation of the divine acquires a kind of "sacramental" image which has not had time to become an esthetic object. All the important imagery of the divine was created in this period. Each people has its own primitive mythological stage, but that of Hellas spans all others in the west and initiates the themes whose variations are heard not only in the roman and medieval periods, the humanistic and baroque, but even in certain corners of existentialism. We

136

meet again and again with Antigone, with Prometheus; we constantly see the great artists at pains to feel in unison with this creative source. And though the later form may be remote from the original, and thus questionable, how much does it still contain if through it (as in Wagner's great work) the primitive imagery shines forth!

It is the great merit of Gerhard Nebel[1] to have brought out the connection between this period of art and christian revelation—going against all the rigid traditions of protestant theology but compelled by the facts—and to have established a real analogy between revelation and the beautiful, both the natural revelation of mythology and the supernatural revelation. The positive results in this outstanding work are all welcome, but not the extreme conclusion that all that is not part of the original event is to be considered a lapse into immanentism and simply vain estheticism and antiquated museum culture. According to Nebel the event cannot extend its range, and the analogia entis remains on the plane of the event. The immanent elements of the beautiful, on which classical esthetics dwelled by preference, are unimportant. Harmony as such, apart from any intervention from above, would be sheer boredom, play merely distraction from self, drama merely horrible, culture a cloak for unpleasant reality. Protestant thought pours scorn upon the various forms which diverge from the original experience, not satisfied until all are leveled out and exploited by positivism and psychoanalysis. If the world is sinful and under judgment then everything under the clouds, high and low, valuable or worthless, is equal. The clouds are broken only

[1] *Das Ereignis des Schönen,* Stuttgart 1953; see also *Weltangst und Götterzorn* 1951.

by the rays of grace from above and, strangely enough, by the beauty of myth, a beauty which is a kind of sign outside history of the grace, the latter being an historical reality; it is thus a real yet most precarious promise, open to all kinds of misuse. Is there then no christian art? There is indeed, through the grace of the power of myth continuing to exert itself in antiquity and the middle ages, but when it finally ceases christian art, a merciful, temporary concession on the part of Christ the judge, has finally become unreal and dead.

The light of the transcendentals, unity, truth, goodness and beauty, a light at one with the light of philosophy, can only shine if it is undivided. A transcendence of beauty alone is not viable; even when it is placed in a close (dialectical) relationship with the christian revelation it is still indebted to the modern esthetic nonmetaphysic of Schopenhauer (however paradoxical this may appear in view of Nebel's thesis). To existentialize beauty on theological grounds would be to prevent its incorporation into the structure of essences, of subjects and objects and their intertwining. We would then be deprived of the possibility of attaining, from our contact with any kind of pure essence, a flower for example, to a genuine original experience of beauty which, through its religious roots, might reach to the same depth of reality as the great mythology brought to birth at its due time in history. This brings home to us that an apparent enthusiasm for the beautiful is mere idle talk when divorced from the sense of a divine summons to change one's life. At the same time the event of the beautiful is not to be held utterly transcendent, as if it derived solely from outside and above. To ascribe such an event to

138

"being" while detaching it from the "coming to be" would be to annul metaphysics by the very act which seeks to establish it. Admittedly it is very difficult to retain the two dimensions simultaneously, that of the transcendent event impinging from above and that of an immanent object bound up with a certain structure. All the compromises in catholic thought thus stop short of this parallelism. The end will be an overemphasis of the structural aspect and a neo-thomist philosophy absorbing scripture into itself. But the difficulty must be faced: the esthetic as a certain structure and the esthetic as experience must be equally taken into account. For this proposition supplies the foundation on which to build a philosophy of the beautiful; it also points to the task before theology.

Art in the christian era is possible as long as the sphere of mythology is still attainable, as long as there are still "gods" in this world. In early christianity the Pantocrator, surrounded by his angels and saints, took over directly the role which in the *Timaeus* is ascribed to the higher godlike beings, a transition we can follow almost step by step from Proclus to Denis the Areopagite. The latter (together with Augustine who, like Boethius in the *Consolation,* took over the inheritance of Plotinus) was the spiritual father of Scotus Erigena; and he, the single esthetic philosopher of the early middle ages, had a far greater influence than is usually thought on the great medieval syntheses, right up to the renaissance, when the kind of intimations associated with neo-platonism were once more in vogue. In the baroque period the gods and the saints often seem to be put on an equal footing in art, and this is not, as is commonly assumed, entirely due to a dramatic convention as regards

139

the former. Admittedly they are assigned only a derivative
splendor, while on the saints fall the rays of a primordial
beauty. Yet neither Winckelmann nor Shelley, Keats,
Hölderlin, nor Goethe in the second part of *Faust,* could
have invoked the world of the gods so ardently if these
bridges spanning the centuries had really been destroyed.
But the structure they envisaged was already toppling, having been erected on a void, a void which has since been
widened through the prevalence of a world view centered
on man which has swept away the last traces of the gods, and
through the transformation of metaphysics into technology
and psychology. The moon, which for Goethe was the symbol of man's purest emotions and, in his portrayal of the classical Walpurgisnacht, the scene of the wild revelry of the
love powers of the universe, is now merely a target for
american and russian missiles. This is called demytholo-
gizing but it is much more. It is in fact the elimination of
the sacred and the loss of the "power of the heart"
(Siewerth) to sense the "majesty of being" (Hans André)
in the immediacy of God. Our concern is not to retain and
transmit the old imagery of the gods but to regain the power
which enabled men to embody the revelation of reality in
the various myths. One must credit christians with this
power, and them alone, for the world which otherwise has
no Godward tendency (since it has become mere matter,
an accumulation of facts, and its synthesis is man in his
state of wretchedness) has for the christian something of
eternity. In its head it has already emerged into the divine
light, and the church glorious in heaven, suffering in purga-
tory and struggling on earth is a single body; the individual
christian too is conscious of sharing in the continual trans-

140

formation from the darkness of this world into the light of the next. What ultimately decides if the salvation proclaimed is the true one is the fact that it does not merely come down from above on a lost world, ripe for judgment, but rather acts upon it. God's grace in fact is bestowed on the world so that, filled with divine power, it may—groaningly and in pain—struggle through into the light of eternity.

The beautiful then will only return to us if the power of the christian heart intervenes so strongly between the other world salvation of theology and the present world lost in positivism as to experience the cosmos as the revelation of an infinity of grace and love—not merely to believe but to experience it. That Dante, Shakespeare and Calderon could do so is clear, but what is strange is that even Eichendorff and Runge could not, in their crumbling world, speak of the miraculous Mozart who, cut off by an impenetrable wall of convention from every authentic world of myth, had the "power of the heart" to sense infallibly the true and the genuine, thereby elevating the conventional to a higher plane and imparting to the whole of created being an overtone at once christian and cosmic. Hopkins too in his obscure fashion effected the same dual resonance in that he linked up the *Spiritual Exercises* with the true myths of creation. Claudel's world, which he considered catholic and often suspected of being unconsciously pagan (see *Claudel* by Robert Grosche), a world of nature and grace, heaven and earth, bible and nature, eros and caritas, joy in creation and desire in abandonment, love for the finite and love for the infinite, sober pursuit of knowledge and mystical love for the mystery beyond understanding—such a

141

world in our day can only be the product of a powerful christian intuition springing from the heart. No one else in our age has given so complete an assent to being in its totality—and this regardless of whatever the existentialists may have to reproach him for. And with him stands Charles Péguy who, though his sweep is less comprehensive, shows even more "power of the heart" in the way he welds together the "pagan and christian soul." His poetry is really prayer and a monologue of the love of God the father as he views the world he created with his dead son in its center, covered with the soft shroud of night . . .

The revelation of beauty must not be confined to the moment when myth exercises its overwhelming power. This is not what Hölderlin means when he says: "Go down, bright sun; they noticed thee too little, they knew thee not, thou holy one." He means the power of the heart today, the power that Hyperion[1] sought in contemporary Hellas and failed to find. The universal night that begins to spread over Hölderlin's Germania is precisely that foretold in the gospel: "The love of many will grow cold." Certainly the present time is one where love is absent, where things are deprived of the splendor reflected from eternity. Even for christians it is extremely difficult to avoid the contagion and not to fall into a kind of eschatological spiritualism which abandons the world to the "powers," which views all that pertains to it in a positivist and neutral light, and which betakes itself to suffering and prayer; this is the danger with Bernanos and Reinhold Schneider in their preoccupation with darkness. Yet it is just as difficult to sense in the spirit of the age what good may arise and withstand

---

[1] In Hölderlin's novel *Hyperion*—tr.

the forces of decline. Abstract art cannot be denied some power of true revelation, although art and earthly beauty cannot be completely divorced from a relationship with man and his living organic image, for he is its center as image and likeness of God. Nonetheless there is a kind of sacral abstraction, that of the Holy Spirit, something in the order of grace that corresponds to what Plato envisaged in his divine world of numbers. This is, basically, beyond both the concrete and the abstract, just as the risen Christ ceased to be concrete as regards the world of history and yet became universalized, having always the power to actualize himself in the most concrete things of history. What is difficult for us need not be impossible; its very difficulty in fact is a call to execute our task with christian generosity.

Created being would not be an image and "outflow" (Thomas) of the sovereign and living God if its transcendentals were static properties, clear and evident to our view, or if, despite their immanence in all contingent beings, they did not have something of the freedom and mysterious depths of God's decision to reveal himself. And since for God creation was to be the first stage of his self-giving to the creature the latter as such retains something of the unfinished character of that early stage, though this does not (as protestant theology maintains) imply, in its contrast with the final completed stage, a general category of revelation, into which the revelation by word falls as a special case. For the transcendentals are not categories of being. The unfinished character of created truth, beauty and goodness is not related to the historical revelation as abstract to concrete, even if the formal quality of openness to God, as opposed to the fulfillment of this openness of God's free intervention,

143

is easily confused with abstractness. But this openness, which belongs to the sphere of created beings, insofar as it is always something other than the ens commune (the sum of realized things which as such are subject to investigation by the understanding) and other than the potentialities hidden in these real essences and thus inexhaustible, is ens transcendens (there is no other—the creation is not a "portion" of being but a participation); and this sphere of openness contains, hidden and unfinished, the goods of salvation: peace in God, beatitude and transfiguration, victory over sin, paradise present though concealed, all that the beautiful consoles us with—and without giving us more than a foretaste, an indication of the "wholly other" fulfillment, not far off but already present: there is one among you whom you know not! This openness really belongs to the world as such and must not be considered supernaturalized; it is the dwelling place of the "gods," the home of genius and of the true experience of those who genuinely encounter them.

3

The esthetic element in revelation

We now have to treat of certain matters that imply an opposite conclusion to the one already suggested. We spoke of the "shock" and repulsion that alone carry man over from the esthetic to the christian sphere. In Israel everything "mystical" was uprooted and discarded to make room for the living God. There was never any transfiguration; the

144

order of grace was perceptible only in the absolute sobriety of the mind. "The world of the new testament," says Nebel, "is completely lacking in the beautiful," and to support this thesis he goes on to say: "David and Solomon were great kings, but art always seeks the proximity of the great powers of history. The galileans, among whom the divine word was made flesh, were provincial, without culture. . . . It is unthinkable that anything beautiful could arise here."

It is true of course that the event with which the scriptural revelation pierces into history impinges so sharply as to come first only as a shock, and that only after it has been received, obeyed and acted upon does it reveal its full breadth and depth. The word is sweet in the mouth but bitter when swallowed. This fact however is acknowledged by christian contemplation and theology, to which the Holy Spirit discloses the power of the divine unity, truth, goodness and beauty, a power secretly present in the event and bursting out into the infinite. Yet it must not be forgotten that the joy of contemplation, surpassing all earthly joys— the frui of passive reception to which Mary of Bethany abandoned herself and which the fathers and medieval writers deemed a foretaste of heaven—is not, despite what Christ said about the "one thing necessary," the direct object of the incarnation. Rather its end is the perfect following of Christ, the faith and loyalty which lead to the cross (counter to human will) and so something which goes beyond contemplation, so gratifying is it. Consequently when contemplation is part of this following, as with the Carmelites, and not simply a consolation and help toward it, it is largely deprived of its savor and becomes an element in the economy of the redemption, an act performed

145

for the church and the world. The cross is the first aim of the incarnation, indispensable as long as the world continues, and whatever share is given in the joy of the resurrection it cannot replace the duty of finding redemption through the cross and of sharing deeply in the passion itself. For this reason, the glory inherent in God's revelation, its fulfillment beyond measure of all possible esthetic ideas, must perforce remain hidden from the eyes of all, both believers and unbelievers, though in very various degrees.

When Paul speaks of Christ's emptying himself, of hiding his glory and becoming poor, and of how his disciples must forego honor and choose opprobrium, become fools for Christ's sake, weak, despised, exiles, and when John promises them the world's hate, they are only expressing how the glory belonging to Christ is done away with; their words do not mean the elimination of the transcendentals of this world, truth, goodness and beauty, in favor of their contraries. Almost the only occasion on which scripture uses esthetic terms is when speaking of the mystery of the suffering servant, and then but to deny their application: "There is in him no eidos and no doxa; we knew him, but he had neither eidos nor kallos;" but this mystery is not something ugly, any more than the veiling of his truth is untruth. "For the foolishness of God is wiser than men, and the weakness of God is stronger than men" (1 Cor 1:25). Thus, insofar as the veil over the face of Christ's mystery is drawn aside, and insofar as the economy of grace allows, christian contemplation can marvel, in the self-emptying of divine love, at the exceeding wisdom, truth and beauty inherent there. But it is only in this self-emptying that they can be contemplated, for it is the source whence the glory

146

contemplated by the angels and the saints radiates into
eternal life. There are "things on which the angels delight
to gaze" (see 1 Pt 1:12), and which "the manifold wisdom
of God makes known to the principalities and powers in
heavenly places through the church" (Eph 3:10). And if
on the first sabbath God is said to have stood back from
his work and contemplated its utter rightness and goodness,
so likewise the great sabbath at the end of time, to which
everything strives (Heb 4:1–10), will be a participation in
the divine contemplation of his works (not only of God but,
with God, of what God has done). The history of revelation then is inevitably interspersed with points of rest which
like the sabbath should grant us a true vision of the course
of divine revelation. If there were no such contemplation
God's revelation would not in fact be worthy of man.
Contemplation of the mystery of the cross does not do away
with the revelation of being (and so of the esthetic factor),
nor does it replace the latter, for then God would be cancel-
ing his own plan for the world, together with the conditions
he laid down for its fulfillment. On the contrary the paradoxical events with which God "shocks" sinful man are
seen as an invitation and stimulus to overleap the bounds
of a closed world of finite ideas and to share in God's self-
manifestation and openness, something to which the creaturely condition itself points, though unable to attain it. It
was the usual tendency of psychology and sociology to
usurp the place of philosophy, a tendency which led
Nietzsche to regard the paradoxes of the new testament as
substituting a proletarian religion for a religion of nobility
and explaining it as an outcome of ressentiment. But it only
needs an unprejudiced view of the facts to realize that the

147

humiliation of the servant only makes the concealed glory shine more resplendently, and the descent into the ordinary and commonplace brings out the uniqueness of him who so abased himself.

The beauty of this event cannot be contemplated from a point outside revelation or alien to it since, as we have seen, revelation itself is interpenetrated with this kind of contemplative vision, between which and the event no hard and fast line can be drawn. Thus in the old testament each new stage presupposes an understanding and contemplative view of the preceding. What has been done takes in the psalms the form of prayer; in the sapiential books they are the object of a contemplation which recapitulates the history while applying and interpreting it. Again, the life of Christ is a recapitulation on the absolute plane of the entire old covenant, and from the high point of the cross and resurrection the whole meaning of his life is expounded before the church for her to keep in memory: " 'These are the words which I spoke to you while I was yet with you, that all things must be fulfilled that are written in the law of Moses and the prophets and the psalms concerning me.' Then he opened their minds, that they might understand the scriptures. And he said to them: 'Thus it is written, and thus the Christ should suffer, and should rise again from the dead the third day' " (Lk 24:44–46). Within this setting of a general worldview come all the various and very personal ways of contemplation: that of Paul who from his own personal experience of grace explains its reversal of a given situation; that of John, the son of thunder, who without violating the old testament scheme of judgment clarifies it by means of the dialectic of love; the author of the epistle to the Hebrews who, raising the old testament "wisdom" to a higher plane, adopts the platonist scheme of shadow and archetype (the basic idea of all esthetic theory) in order to explain the economy of the two testaments; finally the Apocalypse, which transposes the whole concatenation of events of historical revelation onto the plane of vision (imagination working the transformation) and, with the intimation of a fullness of meaning not to be mastered on earth, flies with the "eternal gospel through the midst of heaven" (Ap 14:6).

Thus revelation itself is the foundation of a dialectic, of ever increasing range and intensity, between event and vision, in which the element of the tremendous, inherent in the event itself, nevertheless overwhelms the person contemplating it and then to such a degree that he is left with no alternative than a return to simple discipleship, and this in turn brings a new sense of being overwhelmed, but at a deeper level. This dialectic needs a real structure if it is to be conformable to man and the world. Only such a structure brings out clearly the background of infinite mystery that seeks to reveal itself as the beautiful, true and good. In its absence faith would not be conformable to human nature; it would be spiritualistic and irrational. The historical revelation is molded throughout into a single structure, so that the person contemplating it perceives, through the relationships and proportion of its various parts, the divine rightness of the whole. For however clear and convincing these relationships are they are inexhaustible—not only in the practical sense, because we lack the power to grasp them in their entirety, but also in principle, because what comes to light in the structure is something which opens our minds to the infinite. Contemplation of the historical revelation through the word of scripture then is anything but a "science" on the level of other human "exact" sciences, or even on the level of exegesis, if this means simply the application of the general laws of philology to the special case of the bible. Of course it requires this "exact" method also, provided this latter remembers that "exactness" in a method means the suitability of the method for its object, and that in this case the human, earthly aspect of the object cannot, even in the smallest matter, be isolated and treated on its own and then later be incorporated into the theological vein. The decision for faith cuts right into philology and makes us see in the text a variety of meanings on different levels. The Holy Spirit of the father has "hidden these things from the wise and the prudent and revealed them to little ones;" and it would be a reversion to the error of the scribes to assert that he only discloses the meaning of scripture to the believer by using the findings of modern exegesis, and that any mode of contemplation which receives the divine word without the aid of scientific method cannot bring an adequate understanding of it, however much "pious edification" it achieves. It would be truer to say that philology works for the benefit of the contemplation of the church as a whole, in which the individual directly participates and so in some measure shares in the outcome of its investigations. The Holy Spirit however imparts what is perhaps best designated as a supernatural esthetic sense. This surveys the whole complex of relationships as intended by God; and these have their own

150

power of conviction, by which the revelation of divine things is seen as proving itself.

The center of the whole structure of revelation is the persisting but ever changing relationship between promise and fulfillment, like a diptych displaying on left and right an interaction of features, the one explaining the other and showing its rightness. This applies in the first place to the orders of creation and of grace in general. Within the order of grace it proceeds to the basic relationship of the old and new testaments, a relationship which in turn passes over into the relationship of the two aeons, that of the world which passes and that of its enduring form with God. Each of these diptychs seems, taken by itself, to be fully comprehensible, but the way one merges into another contradicts this appearance and opens up a perspective onto the infinite, where all the results achieved in an earthly sense are canceled, though this does not mean that the individual elements are destroyed or their prophetic meaning disavowed.

Christ, God's greatest work of art, is in the unity of God and man the expression both of God's absolute divinity and sovereignty and of the perfect creature. He is moreover the expression of the son of man's humiliation to the status of slave of the lord and, by this very fact of his elevation as God's son, to the status of coruler with the father. In this divine and human double unity God reveals himself as the eternal two-and-one, father and son in the unity of the Holy Spirit. Thus the christological structure becomes the manifestation of the trinity; in this one human voice also sounds the voice of the father. Whoever has the power to receive in faith this voice with its twofold resonance thereby possesses the interior proof of its rightness (Jn 8:16–17).

This would be a "perception of form" on the highest plane, but because of man's weakness and the difficulty in making the creation, involved as it is in Christ's humanity, participate in this supreme relationship, the vertical dimension is presented horizontally, as extended in time. The son's utterance is now understood as a lifelong obedience to the father's law promulgated on Sinai and to the prophecies made about him. The whole history recorded in the old testament issues in this simple obedience of his which, in thus fulfilling it, makes clear at last how the whole complex network is designed for a definite end; it is like the intricate anatomy of the eye or the ear, one which becomes intelligible when we know what simple seeing or hearing means. One can never manage, by infinitesimal approximation, to smooth out the transition from matter to the act of the senses; there is always a leap, though effected in innumerable stages. In the same way the leap from the old to the new testament is effected by almost infinitesimal degrees (as the present Qumran problems have made us acutely aware) without making Christ's personality, sovereign and free, in the least dependent on any preceding stage. The vertical aspect, that in a man's voice the very voice of God is to be heard, that God speaks along with him, is the culmination of all religion; the horizontal aspect, that fulfillment corresponds to promise, is the culmination of all art. But the extravagance of the fulfillment, the "shock" of the word becoming flesh—an event so revolutionary that it surpasses all possible anticipation—this very extravagance constitutes together with the promise a single *form*. For this reason the unity of the divine and human must also be considered as form, in fact the form of all forms.[1] The diptych pattern persists throughout, corresponding to the duality given in the creation and governing it (Sir 33:7–15) in all the changes history brings as it unfolds its true meaning, for the duality does not imply a static condition. In Christ all that is implied in creation is brought to fulfillment, and so he is one with the church as his creation, bride and body; in this two in one the meaning of the world is made finally manifest under the grace of the father as the eternal marriage of the lamb.

Thus the church is situated between the old testament and Christ's second coming, between the passing and the coming aeon, between earth (the creation) and heaven (the place of God). She is a diptych in the most comprehensive sense. But who or what is the church? What sort of interrelationship, what sort of encounter of human and divine sociology, where one and the same individual alternates between being member of the body and spouse of Christ, between his standing apart as a person and his absorption in a common identity? And, resulting from this, what is the mystery of the christian life with the tension it involves between the claims of the person and those of the mission confided to him, a duality deriving from and analogous with the double nature in Christ: "As the father has sent me so also I send you"? It is a life more full of meaning than any other, one which, in disregarding self in the mission (to the point of martyrdom), losing itself in fact, "gains souls;" a life whose mission demands pliability to

[1] The problem raised by the absence of proportion between God and creature (finiti ad infinitum nulla est proportio) and its bearing on Christ is a basic one in Nicholas of Cusa's theology.

153

Christ and his Spirit, formed by submissiveness to events, and in this passio, this θεῖα παθεῖν, attains its highest activity and fruitfulness. This life comprises three facets, for it implies a vision of what is meant by the christian life, a plunge into this life (the experience of it being quite other than was intended), and its insertion into the framework of the church, for the member must follow a law governing the whole body, a law to which it is superior but which enables it to share in the vitality of the whole.

All this, and much else of the same genre, seems at first sight vague and exaggerated, wild and impossible to substantiate, impossible both in theory and practice. It is only in the interior domain of faith, in living experience of the mystery with all its elements, that its rightness is self-evident. Just as when the specific tone values of a picture reveal themselves to the gaze of the expert in their esthetic "logic," though the layman can only see a hodge-podge of lines and blotches. The rapture of this kind of experience in faith is quite different from what is called estheticism, something quite incompatible with the seriousness of the christian life. Nor is it an anticipation of a state only to be attained in eternity, for the rapturous element of the experience is not a fixed pole, but something ever in motion, something always involved in the interplay of the transcendentals. In the christian scheme the joy and rapture experienced by the individual must ever and again be made subservient to the law of suffering on behalf of the community, and consequently the vision accorded to him must constantly submit to being obscured by the ordinary activities of life. In these the good to be done here and now, the sober truth, counteracts all that beguiles and enchants, and

154

the intoxicating variety of perspectives are gathered up into the one thing necessary, whose simplicity comprises everything, and in which without comprehending it we feel ourselves incorporated and enfolded: ". . . careful to keep the unity of the Spirit in the bond of peace. One body and one Spirit, as you are called in one hope of your calling. One lord, one faith, one baptism. One God and father of all, who is above all, and through all, and in us all" (Eph 4: 3–6). All of a sudden only one thing is essential: love. But from its monism everything constantly comes forth new. The simple richness of the one being opens out and discloses all the fullness of its truth, trinitarian, christological, ecclesiological, sacramental and cosmological.

4

The esthetic element in theology

We have already treated of this element by implication. Contemplation exercised on the rich fabric of revelation and its witness, holy scripture, is itself a beginning of theology and impels us to proceed further. We take this word theology in its widest sense, as the understanding of the truth delivered for our belief, and this presupposes the application of reason and a striving to live by it.

The reason of one who lives in and with the church opens itself out to the greatness of the truth, both to the profundity of its mode of revelation and to the clarity of its form. Such a mind is never seduced by the mirage of an infinity devoid of content or by gnostic subtleties. God's

155

revelation in Christ can have no further relationship with an abstract divine absolute, not even as a matter of speculation or hypothesis, since God has freely decided, from and for eternity, not to be without a world. In it he wills to be glorified and, in order to fill it with his glory, he descended into the abyss of creaturely helplessness, down to the cross and to hades. Consequently we can encounter the deep mystery of God nowhere else but in the context of the world it informs. It is difficult to speak in appropriate terms of the concealment of all form (eidos) and of all rationality in the cross and hades, for the redeemer took upon himself the formlessness of the world's sin so that he might bear it alone and impart to us in its place his own form, christological and ecclesial; and yet this gift must contain (without impairing this form) something of the formlessness of the cross, though as a mystery of the transformation wrought in grace and mercy—it is formlessness created and maintained by the form.

Catholic theology has always been conscious of being subject to the exigencies of the form of Christ. It has always been, at its height, a spiritual activity, aware not only of a rational and ethical but of an esthetic responsibility to the relative proportions of the various parts of revelation. How clearly we see this in the letter of Pope Clement, in its nobility and beauty a prototype of every subsequent encyclical; there we see due measure and love in a unity reflecting the mind of the divine shepherd himself. Justin and Eusebius saw the inner relation between the initial and the perfected stages of revelation in that between creation and history. Irenaeus constructed his theology on the basis of the antiheretical diptych of the old and new testaments

156

and so arrived at the ecclesiastical aspect which dominated his entire thought. And so it continues. It is easy to see how the inner form of the bible, transmitted through the form of the church, puts its imprint on all these systems of theology, however original and personal they may be. Perhaps we should even speak of its hellenistic imprint, with its proclivity for the beauty of myth, its mundane flavor, its domestication of the mystery of sin and redemption. Once again let us hear what protestantism has to say: "Anyone who is concerned with the world in all its range, with forms and proportions, with man's heroism, with morality, with the splendor of forms, with the exploration of the sphere of myth, will feel repelled by protestantism. Luther destroyed the rich treasury of myth, and replaced it with an arid, official Institute. Anyone enamored of beauty will shiver in the barn of the reformation, just as Winckelmann did, and feel the pull of Rome."[1] The warning given here must be attended to. But the contrast drawn leaves out the factor of contemplation and also its basis, the proportion inherent in revelation itself, which refuses to let the event, by its own impact, dominate and exclude all the rest, but joins event and form together, indissolubly. This, we feel, is what is lacking in Luther.

Catholic theology must not of course be sought exclusively in the beautifully elaborated systems of Augustine, Bonaventure and Thomas Aquinas. No less important is the theologically formed existence of all those disciples and confessors whose concern was never to set themselves up as christian personalities but rather solely to follow the christian life in forgetfulness of self. The concept of a

[1] See Nebel, op. cit. 188.

"theological existence" has a scriptural basis for, in both the old and new testaments, those entrusted with certain tasks sacrificed their own private existences in order to be the bearers of revelation. The last part of the gospel of John for example can only be understood if we take Peter and John both as persons and as office holders, that is, as "real symbols" of the church in her authority and her love; and a similar consideration applies to the other two "pillars of the church," James and Paul. In their sharply contrasting roles they were not engaged in personal conflict, but embodied the dialectic of one function with another. For the unity of the church is a supernatural one and not definable in earthly terms; and it can only be realized in a surrender, ventured in faith, to the office actually committed to her, or rather in the still higher venture wherein different offices alternately come together and contrast in a common surrender to the church which comprises all. The basic experience recorded in the Acts of the Apostles is continued at various levels throughout the history of the church. The latter is not a continuance of revelation (which finished with the apostles), nor is it a kind of secular history of no concern to revelation (a history of christian communities and individuals). It consists essentially in a continuous embodiment of the son's life, through the Holy Spirit, in innumerable forms of participation. These are variations on the theme, bringing to light all its latent possibilities, showing how all life and history is penetrated and informed by the original form of Christ.

What is distinctively catholic is that this informed existence is posited within the objective, prescribed and, for the individual subject, normative form of the church. The

158

hierarchical office is a form, the sacramental system is a form; and obedience to the church according to her mind is how the individual appropriates the form. Whatever heights he may be called to in his choices and decisions his life is, from the outset, made significant by reason of an attitude informing everything, an attitude which ultimately derives from the attitude of the church as bride of Christ, and of her archetype, the "handmaid of the lord." Even the believer finds it astonishing that the real life of faith continues to be lived, upheld by the grace of God. It is, at its highest, the mystery of the cross, of the mystical night of faith which, with all its terrors and feelings of abandonment, cannot shake for a moment the loyalty of the lover. He remains enclosed and protected within an unbreakable, crystalline form.

The content of this form is the father's gift to us of agape, flowing out in the nuptial love between Christ and the church, a love which can certainly be called eros in its highest and most original sense. The Canticle of Canticles, in its clear erotic import, is prophetic of this its fulfillment, whether it be taken or not as applicable, in the meantime, to the nuptial love between yahweh and his people. And in any case its literal sense is not to be given so sacred a significance as to make it, from the very beginning, a "play of mysteries," thereby depriving the words of their plain meaning. For it is not mainly a question of particular concrete statements open to allegorical interpretation but of the creation of a highly charged erotic atmosphere, which alone gives force to the words and acts of the king, of the sunamitess and the incidental characters. The whole setting is redolent of the harem of an oriental potentate but the sunamitess, as is frequently insisted, is unique among the thousand chosen, the spotless one; what takes place is presented as in singular contrast with the pervading atmosphere. It was written after the religion of yahweh had begun to establish itself and to uproot all the other religions with their erotic and orgiastic practices; it was too about the time of Solomon's downfall into the idolatry of the canaanites under the impulse of eros. Accordingly this canticle thus interpreted served an indispensable purpose, since human eros (gathering up and sublimating all the eros in nature) is an ingredient of human love, even though the latter has long ceased to have the beguiling atmosphere of eros as its form and prerequisite. Eros, being a mode of love that foreshadows and promises the fulfillment of all earthly love, is not to be discarded as valueless; and since we are concerned with the incarnation and with a nuptial relationship in one flesh in the eucharist, the passion and the resurrection, there can no question of asserting that eros, transformed, may not pass over the threshold of the new testament. The atmosphere of the gospel is admittedly one of sober dedication to the "work" at hand, but with constant reference to the festival day with the bridegroom already present; the frequent feastings, no mere allegorical formalities, are *the* sign of the son of man (Mt 11:19). There is nothing dionysic here, for it is the beginning of the new testament; yet the warmth of God's heart has been reproduced in the warmth of a human heart. Earthly eros as an "atmosphere" blooms but briefly, and every man has the duty to compensate its withering by the force of his love, to endue it, transformed, with renewed vitality through the moral power of the heart. But the mys-

160

terious bond between Christ and the church has something
of eternal youth; the nuptial state is timeless, as that of the
Canticle, where the I-thou relationship does not envisage a
later stage (children and household concerns). Here indeed eros, raised above the various ends it serves in organic
nature, unconcerned with birth, death and worldly strivings,
is set directly on the line leading from the first beginnings
of paradise to the marriage feast at the end of time. The
Canticle is a poetical representation and thus a promise of
a reality that is made present in Christ and the church,
raised above all conflicting purposes and all transience.

Certainly we are taught both by scripture and the great
classical theology to speak of this reality with reserve; yet,
as this same theology also shows, we should apply to it all
the powers of the heart. For in its greatest period theology
cannot be considered apart from the innumerable commen-
taries on the Canticle, as embodying the central mystery of
all theology. The same impulse is given by the great mystical tradition, which cannot be discarded merely because
of a few ambivalent, incidental phenomena or because of
ecstatics like Teresa, or as an insignificant element of the
church's life that is better avoided. Consider only the series
of great commentators on Denis the Areopagite, whose
writings on the mystery of the divine eros are so liturgical
in tone and breathe a spirit of awe and reverence. How
barren seems the modern, academic approach, which has
served to unmask falsifications, in comparison with the
sensus catholicus of the great visionaries and theologians,
so conscious of the continuity between Paul and the Areopagite, between the epistle to the Hebrews and the two
"hierarchies!" The loss of the erotic element of the Canticle

161

and of the esthetic element of the dionysian writings has resulted in a dessication of theology. What it needs is to be steeped anew in the very heart of the love mystery of scripture, and to be remolded by the force it exerts.[1]

The spirituality of the christian artists and esthetic philosophers of the last century (from 1860 to the present) is strongly brought out by their preserving a sense of the unity of beauty and religion, art and religion, when they had hardly any support from theology, and notwithstanding the breakdown of the old tradition and the prevalence of materialistic and psychological views incompatible with theirs. In this they were in accord with the original tradition of the west, as well as with the sentiment of the learned in various countries. For behind them lay, despite the solvent effect of Kierkegaard, the religious force of german idealism, of Goethe, Schelling and Novalis, and this exerted its influence on the England of Coleridge, Newman, Thompson and Hopkins, which in turn was connected by hidden but strong ties with the France of Péguy (as Alexander Dru has shown in his excellent study of the latter). Péguy's religious and poetic insight, in his *Clio, Eve, Mystères* and *Note Conjointe,* surpasses in profundity the tremendous synthesis of Claudel's *Ars Poetica Mundi,* which itself links up Aeschylus and the psalms with Thomas Aquinas and his own very dramatic and individual interpretation of created being. Claudel the artist did not shrink from helping to fill up certain gaps in modern exegesis by making his own commentary on the Canticle. Maritain and Gilson have both placed the esthetic of the great scholastics in the set-

[1] "No divine quality has, perhaps, been so neglected" as beauty. See Pohle-Gierens *Dogmatik* I, 9, 213–14.

ting of present-day problems, and the extraordinary range of writers dealt with in the work of Edgar de Bruynes (*Etudes d'esthétique médiévale*, three vols) makes it impossible to ignore such a wealth of speculation. Manzoni in Italy, Soloviev in Russia, Lotze in Germany, the schools of christian theists, Haecker in his later work, Adolf Dyroff, Rilke too in his conception of inspiration, all maintain the same general outlook. The fact that so many creative artists (almost all composers and many painters) turn back in their maturity to the profundities of revelation is significant of the coming of an attitude totally different from that which previously prevailed.

Beauty is not subject to man's command, and nothing is freer, less subject to hard and fast rules than the balance between the favorable historical circumstances in which great art appears and the freedom of divine grace. The latter is not there for the purpose of compensating the lack of the former. Nonetheless the prayer of the artist for the right spirit and the right kind of inspiration has always been effective. No matter how great the genius he can no longer, now that the mystery of Christ has come to dwell with us, penetrate to the heart of beauty without the aid of the Holy Spirit. If both cannot be conjoined perfectly—the gospel is no human work of art—it is always the function of a given epoch to make itself receptive to the art of the Holy Spirit, to let the power of love mold it, for it is the absence of this that explains the coldness of our own art; that fire alone can rekindle it. Only one whose heart is attuned to the art of God can be expected to establish order and due proportion in the confusion and chaos of the present.

163

THE WORD AND SILENCE

Verbo crescente verba deficiunt

In all religions men come to be sated with words and attracted to the charm of silence. Words form part of the clamor of the world; they are essentially delimiting, denominating, defining, determining. They express the law of essences and become themselves a law, a positive ordinance. Whether they set out to encompass truth in its finite form or, as the true way of the law, dhammapada, to point toward truth, the sharp edges of the finite hurt the finite creature, who hankers after perfect liberation from restriction, after the nameless. "The name is sound and smoke, overclouding heaven's brightness." For surely in every finite manifestation is shown forth the one that is not to be counted as one among the many. The being in which all is immersed is truly no abstraction; it is act and reality, and every individual thing speaks of it, without its content being exhausted. The "nothing of all that" is what the finite hungers and thirsts for, and the name we attach to it is of no consequence; its blessedness consists in being unnamable. In Asia more than elsewhere men have turned their face toward this mysterium fascinosum, and as we have said it

165

matters little whether the way leading to it is conceived as a "revealed religion" in which a ray from beyond pierces through to enlighten and guide the votary in his attainment of a mystical nirvana, or the way is followed out as an ascetical technique of liberation from all the finite and of stripping away all the coverings of being. The aim in both cases is the same. For even the revelation of a God who redeems can, from the standpoint of this purpose, be held as no more than subsidiary and transient, one avatar among others. But the religious yearnings of Asia are the root whence spring the great european religions and world-views. The enlightenment itself, Hamann, Herder and the romantics not only sensed but actually knew how indebted Greece was to the east, knew the unity of the whole eastern Mediterranean. The spiritual formation of the west was due to a Syrian (Denis the Areopagite), an Egyptian (Plotinus), an African (Augustine); and we know how the sense of longing it caught from the east constantly spurred the west to new crusading zeal, both in the physical and spiritual spheres.

In fact man's last word is one of repudiating his own words. Virgil in his will left instructions to burn his *Aeneid*. Thomas ceased to write some time before his death; all that he had written seemed so much straw. At the age of forty-three Gogol threw the second and third volumes of *Dead Souls* into the fire, and died a few days later. How many fires must have blazed like that on the eve of death, destroying what the author, freed at last, willed "to know no longer according to the flesh," all part of the holocaust wherein he achieved his own transformation? What can escape being destroyed along with all the rest? Nothing—except, for

166

a christian, the word of God as set down by him. Verba mea non transibunt, not even in the final conflagration of heaven and earth. The earth sinks, the heavens dissolve, the sea turns to vapor, but the eagle flies through the midst of heaven, in his beak the scroll of the evangelium eternum.

There comes a time for the christian when he wearies of all that is positive and concrete. He finds himself enchained by words and facts, without hope of liberation. In all other religions the finite is seen sooner or later to point beyond itself, to be an intermediary. Even for the poet who loved the finite world so much there came a time when he sang the praises of the living things that aspired to death by fire, when he himself wished for the moment when, in the first glimpse of eternal life, we lose sight of ourselves. For the christian however the positive and concrete persist to the end, and isolate him from the rest of mankind. This is true both of catholics and protestants. The catholic appears more confined by the sacraments in their character of a definite event (a character diminished in protestantism, which tends to regard them as mere memorials of a single, eternal event), by the positive character of the hierarchical institution, dogmatic formularies, laws and prescriptions, from which he can never be liberated all his life, and which give his life (viewed from the standpoint of what is highest in religion) the character of a penitential progress. The protestant is confined more stringently by the positive character of the word of scripture, which he wills to be all sufficient, without any mysticism to soften its rigidity, without any contemplation to transfigure its sense, without the principle

167

of tradition to make it more attractive. As his own judge of the bible he files away at the chain he himself has forged, torn in opposite directions by faith and reason, by the Christ of faith and the Jesus of history. Neither catholicism nor protestantism can ever make its message more attractive to mankind by freeing it from the positivity of the word in its historical factual character, whether by transforming it in a moral, ascetical sense or in a mystical and contemplative sense. Missionaries of other religions have their books which they propagate and expound, and it is a source of humiliation for the christian missionary not only that he has to begin with a book but that he must always continue with it; he can never lay it aside as finished with. "God's word says this, forbids that—see Luke, chapter and verse so-and-so." Indeed it is perfectly true that the God of Abraham, Isaac and Jacob proclaims himself as the true God, present to the world, no otherwise than with these positive, historical credentials and under this name. He is the God whose will it was to rouse the attention of his people of old with repeated new, unexpected positive revelations and instructions, and who has fettered his new people with the positive revelation of his son, never to be superseded: "Hear him;" while the son for his part has fettered his followers with the positivity of the church: "He that hears you hears me." How can a religion so enchained to what is positive and concrete hope to still the yearning of men's hearts for what is without name? The voice of one sated with words is heard even in the bible: "Of making many books there is no end, and much study is an affliction of the flesh" (Eccl 12:12).

Truly "the letter kills." Has Christ then, and what he

brought into the world and inaugurated, killed the letter? What did Paul mean by saying: "And if we have known Christ according to the flesh, but now we know him so no longer" (2 Cor 5:16)? Can there be for the christian a stage beyond history and the word as set down? Is not all that is positive made merely provisional through the doctrine of the resurrection, by which the flesh is not destroyed but "transfigured," and which replaces the desire for absorption in God by the desire that the temporal be made eternal? "For we would not be unclothed, but clothed upon;" "Yet so that we be found clothed, not naked;" "For we know, if our earthly house of this habitation be dissolved, we have a building of God, . . ." (2 Cor 5: 1–4). Yet it is still a question of a building, a heavenly Jerusalem, whose walls have been measured, though by angels, with streets, real streets, though of gold and transparent like glass. And if its temple is now God, the almighty lord, it is also the lamb; and if the lord remains invisible on his throne the lamb itself is visible. And how many transcendent events are depicted in the Apocalypse!

"But the Spirit quickeneth," the Spirit, that is, of God who makes use of the syllables of a divine revelation in a way analogous to the use made by the poet of a language already in existence to express in his own way what is beyond speech, analogous also to the mystic's constant attempt in words to convey what he has learned in silence. "But the lord is Spirit," even insofar as he is the word of God. For granted that he was the word of the "nonword" and that his word was to be understood, would it not need to be understood, necessarily, as the word of the "nonword?" Would not the language of the "positivity" of the

169

christian revelation (which is not the same as that of
created nature in general) have to be taken as the expression of something which is itself neither "speech" nor
"expression," and what may very well be the *truth* of what
all human religion strives after, though it exceeds man's
grasp?

1

Immediately after the apostolic period, beginning with Ignatius of Antioch, silence is seen as superior to the word. The
expressions he uses are so pointed and definite that they
have never been superseded, indeed hardly equalled by any
christian writer.

"It is better to be silent and to be than to speak and not
to be. To teach is good, if one does what one says. There
is one teacher, who spoke and it was done; and what he did
in silence ranks on a level with the father. Whoever really
possesses the word of Jesus can sense also his silence, how
he is perfect, how he works through his word, and is known
through his silence" (*Eph* 15:1–2). The word of Jesus
sounds from out a place of silence for it to be a word at all.
That place is, firstly, the silence of the father, "who has revealed himself through his son, Jesus Christ, who is his word
come forth from silence" (*Mag* 8:2). But for this very reason
it is also Christ's own silence, which can be perceived by
the man who has received his word. He is perfect in that,
like Christ himself, he acts by speaking but is known in his
silence, in the greater sphere of mystery; it is there that
the word must be, pervading it in order to be the word of

170

God. This sphere is filled with the silent "doing" and "being" of the word—ultimately his silent suffering. For Ignatius this is the visage presented by the church: "The more I see a bishop keeping silent the greater should be the reverence I have for him" (*Eph* 6:1). "With this bishop I have come to learn that he obtained the services of the community not by his own efforts or through men. . . . I am astounded at his mildness, which can do more by silence than idle words can" (*Philad* 1:1). Interior silence carries the word that sounds, justifies it and gives it efficacy. "The tree is known by its fruit, and those who confess themselves disciples of Christ are visible by their deeds" (*Eph* 14:2). This interior silence is, for Ignatius, love, its unity and harmony, founded on the unity of Jesus with the father; more precisely the unity of faith (God's gift of his unity with us) with love (as living by this unity), the harmony within the church, which harmony is for him *the* word of God to the world (*Mag* 1:4; 6:8). It is not inappropriate that the silence of the love on which every word is founded is depicted in musical images, as the symphony of love, harmony of strings (Eph 4:1–2;5:1). Certainly the mysteries of Christ, his being conceived and born of a virgin, his death on the cross are "three resounding mysteries, that were accomplished in the silence of God" (*Eph* 19:1), but it is not their visibility that is the greatest element: "Yet thereby our God Jesus Christ makes it all the more manifest that he is in the father" (*Rom* 3:3); through his death he has disappeared and returned to the father. Consequently the Romans are not to hinder the death of Ignatius by ill-timed pleas: "For if you are silent about me, I shall be a word; but if you love my flesh, I shall

171

be merely a sound" (*Rom* 2:1). Against the argument that "so is it written" Ignatius points to the living and life-giving word of Christ: "For me the documents of Jesus Christ, the sacred documents, are his cross, death and resurrection" (*Philad* 8:2).

Why should not this be held the authentic experience and interpretation of christianity? Why should gnosticism (with its Sige and Hesychia) have offered more than a mere word, not even a concept? What Ignatius learned by what he experienced was that this positive element, the word as flesh, as resounding speech and as scripture, only has validity, is only understandable in conjunction with the infinite sphere which it witnesses to and reveals, and which is purely and simply the sphere of reality and of realization.

The dispute with the gnostic myth, especially that of Valentine, rules out for christian thought any possibility of designating God primarily as "silence" or "abyss." "Silence is for those the mother of all who come forth from the abyss, and she kept silence about everything she could not say, as inexpressible in words, but what she comprehended she declared beyond understanding" (*Extr ex Theod* 29). Clement, who observed this idea, introduced the theme of the secret mystery into christian theology (*Strom* IV, 177; IV,316); he also drew a parallel between the greek poets' and dramatists' idea of the unknowability of God and the statements of scripture about the "God whom no man has ever seen" (Jn 1:18), about Paul's hearing "secret words which it is not granted to man to utter" (2 Cor 12:4), and about the unfathomable "depths of the riches and the wisdom and knowledge of God" (Rom 11:33), which might well justify the appellation abyss. But it is the

172

incarnate word that frees us from our limited conceptions and introduces us to that in God which surpasses our understanding. "When we have abstracted all that pertains to bodies and to the so called incorporeal things, immersing ourselves in the greatness of Christ, and thence reverently proceeding to the infinite, then we will, in some degree, approach to a perception of the almighty, and come to know, not what he is, but what he is not" (*Strom* V,71,3). This is for Clement the doctrine both of Plato and of Moses, the first step of the negative theology. For the Cappadocians the defense of the incomprehensibility of God against the heresy of Eunomius is the basic concern of christian theology, for "through silence" do we honor the divine excellence, which reveals itself only to faith (*Gr Nyss C Eun* II,105; I, 371). From there it seems but a step to the mystical silence of neo-platonism which, for Proclus, is the condition for the ascent to God; taken over from him by Denis it is no longer the logos but the angels who "proclaim the divine silence" (*Div N* 4,2), and are themselves the reflection of "the goodness of the silence dwelling in the abyss" (4,22). "But of God's peace and stillness, which the holy Justos calls soundlessness (aphthenxia), and his immobility in all his outgoings of which we have cognizance, in what manner this peace is silent and keeps at rest, how he is in himself and is disposed in his inmost being, and is supereminently one in his wholeness, and neither in his going into himself nor in his going out into the many loses his self-unity, but even in his proceeding into the all remains wholly within himself by reason of the superabundance of the unity of being transcending all: to express this,

173

or even to think it, is not possible to any being" (*Div N* 11,1).

It is along this way that greek thought, echoing that of Asia as a whole or simply the longings of mankind, penetrated into christian theology, where it served the purpose of keeping open the spaces of the divine infinity. In the words of the Areopagite one cannot point to anything definitely at variance with the christian idea of God, apart from a certain abstractness, which itself is more suggested to the reader than intended by the writer. The "hierarchies" and the letters show that he did not turn away from the word that is Christ, but tried to reach through its finite form to the infinite form. In this he followed Origen and his doctrine of the inner unity of the word. "The total word of God that was in the beginning with God . . . is something other than words. The one word consists of many and various knowable contents, but . . . none of these words is 'word.' But whoever utters what pertains to the truth, even should he speak about everything and omit nothing, would yet always be saying but a single word. The saints, who hold themselves always to the one word as their end, are not given to much speaking." Thus all the words of scripture are a single word, "since each is gathered up in it as in the one head" (*Orig in Joh* V,4–6). The whole exegesis of Origen is concerned with the achievement of this movement to unity, with bringing out how the living and abiding logos is present in every particle of meaning: in the word lives the superword which was from the beginning. The unremitting movement of ascent on the part of the alexandrian thinker was the outcome of his intense love of Jesus; but should one hesitate to commit himself to it he may well turn to Augus-

174

tine, who taught the same about the silencing of words in the word.

"In the beginning was the word. Only wordlessly can one come to a perception of this; it is not made apparent by the agency of human words. There we have a certain form, a form that is not formed, but the form of all the formed. . . . All is in him, and yet, since he is God, all is under him. We have said what is incomprehensible, what was read; and it was not read that man might understand it, but that it should afflict man because he does not understand it, and he loses himself in going forth into the apprehension of the unchanging word. . . . We speak of God; what wonder, then, if you do not understand? For if you understand, it is not God . . . Groping in the Spirit to touch God is great blessedness, to apprehend him an impossibility. . . . So the word became flesh, to nourish us with the milk of those not yet grown up" (*Serm* 117; *PL* 38, 662–71). The "milk" teaches us the inadequacy of our knowledge, but in this life there is in fact no "solid food." The most solid is the act in which the word became flesh, and this act is a silent word. "Likewise in silence, speaking through the facts themselves, Christ, our lord, says: Wherewith to die I did not possess; thou, man, had not wherewith to live. I took from thee that whereby I might die for thee; take thou from me that whereby thou lives with me. We perform a solemn exchange: I give to thee, give thou to me" (*S Denis* 5,5; *Morin* 26).

For Augustine word and answer between God and man, Christ and the church, exceeds all utterance so greatly that word disappears into wordless jubilation. "When you come near to yourself and begin to sense God thereby (persentis-

175

cere)—according as love grows in you, for God is love—
then you sense something which you say, and yet do not
say. For before you felt it, you intended to say it to God;
now you begin to feel it, and feel that what you feel you
cannot say. But have you learned from this that what you
feel is unsayable; will you then be silent? Will you not
praise? How, then, you say, can I praise? The little that I
perceive, through a glass darkly, I cannot explain. Listen,
then, to the advice of the psalm: Sing joyfully to God, all
the earth! You understand the jubilation of all the earth, if
you also rejoice in the lord. Rejoice in the lord, do not
divide up your rejoicing among different things. In the end,
all the other can be expressed in some way; He alone, who
spoke and all was made, cannot be expressed. He spoke, and
we were made; but we cannot utter him. His word, by which
we were uttered, is his son; in order to be spoken, in some
way, by us, he became weak. By rejoicing, we can answer
his word, but not word for word" (*En in ps* 95, n 5–6).
"What does singing joyfully to him mean? Not to be able
to express in words what is sung in the heart" (32 *en* 2; *s*
1,8). "It is good for you to renounce your self in the praise
of God, better than to advance in self-praise. For if you
praise God, and cannot explain what you want to say, your
thinking is extended inwards, and this extension makes
you stronger in apprehension of him whom you praise"
(145,4). Here he inserts his mysterious sentence about the
Adyton: "Est quasi adytum, quod dicitur penetrale secretum
(*Heb* 9:3), interius templi. Et quid est hoc? Quod solus
sacerdos intrabat. Et forte ipse sacerdos est absconditum
tabernaculum Dei" (26:10). Indeed he is the countenance

176

of God himself: "Abscondes eos in abscondito vultus tui" (30:8).

Augustine also places the whole of philosophy in the very center of his theology; the mysterious way into the interior, followed by philosophy, religion and mysticism, is formed and illuminated all through by what is itself most interior, and only discovered because it reveals itself as word and truth. "God speaks through the truth itself, provided one is capable of hearing it in the Spirit" (*Civ D* XI,2). Consequently for Augustine all the words of revelation come together in a single word, love, which however speaks through deeds rather than words.

The word of Christ, who spoke as no other had spoken, who alone spoke as one having power, is nonetheless an insecure bridge between the wordlessness of the world and the superword of the father. Something of this order was implied by Matilda of Magdeburg when she wrote, at the end of her fourth book: "Then spoke our lord, Jesus Christ: Do thou speak, O father, I will now be silent, as thou art silent in the mouth of thy son, on fire with love, on account of the weakness of men. And my humanity spoke trembling and hesitant on account of the falsehood of the world, but the world repaid me with a bitter death" (IV,28).

Finally Nicholas of Cusa brings together the dialectic of word and superword with that of the descent of the word into the silence of death. "We possess a redeemer, who is a universal mediator, fulfills all things, and is the firstborn of every creature. This Jesus caused, from the beginning of the world, a unique voice to sound in the ears of his redeemed members, a voice gradually swelling until it sounded

177

loudest in himself at the time when he gave up his spirit. This voice proclaims that there is no other life than life in the word, and that the world, as it came forth from the word, keeps in being by the word and is led back to its origin. This return is effected by the subordinate beings, each in their order, being brought back by those that are higher, and the first of all, who brings back all the rest, is Jesus. No one returns to the state of blessedness, unless he discards all stain and disfigurement, and becomes spiritual . . . in the purity of justification. That is the great voice sounding in the depths of our spirit, the voice which the prophets proclaim to us, urging us on to adore the one creator, to practice virtue, to take refuge with the redeemer, by whom we are enabled to transcend the life of the senses. After this voice, having sounded for millennia, had come to John, the voice of one crying in the desert, who pointed with his finger to the redeemer, it took on human form, and, finally, after a long and varied course of teaching and miracles, designed to show us that, of all terrible things, the most terrible is what love must choose, the death of sense, he uttered a loud cry, and so departed" (*Excitat* 1,3).

These few passages may be taken as representative of countless others. They serve to bring out two things: that all the concrete historical facts of the bible go far beyond the facts of secular history (Hegel's starting point in his phenomenology), and possess an inexhaustible significance in the interior sphere; and that this sphere is the proper setting of all mankind's religious perception in philosophy, poetry and ordinary life. Only if we see them in this context we come to a true understanding of the full significance of revelation.

178

2

We can therefore say that the biblical facts possess an external historicity which forms, as it were, the basis of their participation in the actual world history. At the same time this external historicity is the place, the vessel and the physical expression of the real event of revelation, which is by no means merged and dissolved therein. It is strange that of the three that give testimony on earth to the truth, "the Spirit, the water, and the blood" (1 Jn 5:8), none is actually word, but all witness to the word that is Christ: the Spirit as the God who inspires; the water as the active effect of the word, namely the church; the blood, finally, in the moment when the word consummated his work in silence and in a loud, inarticulate cry. In these three consists the main import of the word in its historical course, and all three point to its character as "prehistorical" (das Urgeschichtliche). In speaking of the word as prior to history we do not mean that it is merely above history. We might say that it pervades all history, meaning thereby that we are concerned with an event which took place at a certain historical time, and also, since it comes from God, that it touches the whole of history and every moment of it. The Spirit (as the presence and witness of God in the word of Christ) is what makes it thus primary or all pervasive in history, the water (as sacrament) is the transposition wrought by the Spirit of what took place once into the history of all times, and the blood is (in virtue of the hypostatic union) the event wrought and made permanent by the son himself, a unique event yet ever reiterated. This "triunity" is the

179

firm ground to which all previous revelation in history is directed. It is what unifies the original event of the divine revelation, which is also prehistorical, with the reality consisting of the events of secular history; it makes each presuppose the other if they are to be understood. In it therefore, in the fullest sense, the word is made flesh.

Looking back from this standpoint on the long road leading to this event, on the old testament, we are obliged to say that the unification was there only in prospect, only imaged forth, only in promise. The verbum caro, the unity of what took place once, prior to history, with the continuous process of world history, was only tried out, and not necessarily always in the same way. And since it was a matter of a preliminary exercise, one and the same text for example could be taken up again by later writers, with their deeper experience, and reinterpreted accordingly, just as a pupil when more advanced may go back to and improve on his previous exercises. This brings out clearly that it is not in this instance so much a question of the exact nature of historical events as of the overall "right" expression for the essential, revelatory event embodied in that history. It was in the light of their deeper and clearer understanding that the deuteronomists worked over the Heptateuch, and thus for the first time traced a continuous thread through the scattered traditions of the time of the judges, a primary theological thread, which then, secondarily in narrative form, was presented as an historical thread. Not only in the work of the deuteronomists but even in earlier recensions the historical and narrative was chosen as the most fitting embodiment for a supernatural experience of revelation, a consciousness of revelation. Consequently it is a question

180

neither of abstracting from this narrative form so as to elicit some kind of general truth (as the moral of history), nor of always taking this embodiment for the thing itself, regardless of the difference between the two aspects of history. One may of course adopt, as a measure of prudence, the principle that all that is recorded should be taken as historical truth so long as the contrary is not established on historical and literary grounds, as for instance, with Jonas, Judith and Tobias. But we may well ask whether in recognizing that the book of Jonas is a parable we do not lose some of the substance of revelation, and whether this is not also the case if we must regard, say, the story of Joseph as a purely literary composition, not to mention a great part of the story of the patriarchs, the various episodes of the exodus and of the entrance on the promised land. After all it is hardly likely that we can succeed in isolating from the narrative its "historical core" with a view to comparing the two; and besides it is not only the historical core but the narrative itself that is the object of inspiration and theologically relevant. Why then should we be so zealous for proofs of historicity? We must be quite clear that the main dates of Israel's history are obviously historical, and equally so the facts of its special consciousness of revelation, expressed not only in its acts, conduct, worship and prayer but also in the way it interpreted and described its own history. This is the main consideration and it is not to be discarded, even though we have no need, theologically speaking, to attach particular weight to the historicity of details transmitted through so many and such varied channels. How much in the way of revelatory meaning might be added to a given historical fact! Is this not clearly the case with

181

the episode of Melchisedech. And why should it not apply also to Abraham, though admittedly not quite a parallel case? Nor must we overlook the fact that jewish history, the nearer it comes to the time of Christ, and so the more exact and susceptible of proof it becomes, the less eventful it appears in a theological sense. There was nothing like the same profound theological reflection among the Jews on the history of the Macchabees as there was on the less certain events of their own origins, so pregnant with revelatory significance, or as there was on the times of the kings and the prophets, so conscious were they of the religious import of these. The latest writers, those who added the "deutero-canonical" narratives, were obviously concerned to employ that form which could comprise the deepest and widest theological content.

All this goes to show that from out the historical "form" the prehistorical content is seen steadily rising to an ever greater height, like a mountain range in the background. It means that, through all the words of scripture, despite their inevitable limitations as human words, the *one* word makes itself heard more and more decisively, and that Israel was profoundly conscious of this. Admittedly Israel possessed its national pride and, like any other people, was inclined to dramatize its own history. But its chief concern was to reduce the whole to the single act, at all times incumbent on it, of fidelity in faith to the God who was faithful to his people. This is shown in the compilation of Deuteronomy. This singleness of purpose is what Jesus in fulfilling carried over into the eternal covenant. It is what Paul pointed to in his relegation, as inessential, of the law and even of circumcision, and made everything dependent on the faith of

182

Abraham, the father of all believers, both Jews and gentiles. It is at the same time a relegation of every word insofar as it is not flesh.

But in fact this relegation could only occur when the Holy Spirit came forth from the risen Christ, who proclaimed himself, now become spiritualized in his humanity, as the truth of all salvation history, and of his own life and death history: "These are my words which I spoke to you when I was yet with you" (Lk 24:44). From his own being as spirit he "took away the veil" (2 Cor 3:16) which lay over all the words and narratives of the old and new testaments, hiding their real meaning. This is why Paul was able to bring out the central doctrines of christianity, with a truly astonishing freedom, without citing a single word of the gospel. It explains too how it was that he could make himself responsible for dispensing the gentiles from the tradition contained in the word and history, insofar as this tradition was not in its essence the spirit of God who revealed himself in word and history.

We Christians always fail to appreciate the abruptness of the passage from the old to the new aeon, signified by the son giving up his spirit on the cross (commendo spiritum meum, tradidit spiritum), and by the investiture of the Holy Spirit with all freedom and power over the son's word and flesh. "He shall receive of mine, and shall show it to you" (Jn 16:14), that is to say, of Christ's word and flesh. But one cannot say that the teaching of the Spirit is itself word. It is the "glorification" of the word and so united in the trinity with the word; but the Spirit is not the word. This alone brings home to us what Paul meant when he was emboldened to emancipate the gentiles from

183

the letter, to subject them to the Spirit. It makes us see also that the christian mission to the world today is not one of subjecting the nations to the letter but to the Spirit. Certainly this does not mean the human spirit of religion, philosophy, mysticism, but the divine Spirit, which is itself freedom, far greater and more positive than the freedom of the human religious spirit from matter and the course of history; it is not contrasted with this human freedom as wholly other but takes and includes it within itself. Because of the "freedom wherewith Christ has made us free" (Gal 4:31) "the Spirit of the lord is liberty" (2 Cor 3:17); but this does not mean that those freed have to hear him —it is the word we have to hear—but rather that they are moved, led, inspired by him (Gal 5:18; Rom 8:14), inwardly "minding the things of the Spirit" whose wisdom is "life and peace" (Rom 8:5–6). Everything leads into the *identity* of the Spirit who, on the one hand, is the "Spirit of Christ" (8:9), of him who "raised up Jesus from the dead" (8:11), and so of the father—in short the Spirit of God; and on the other hand who is, in us ourselves, the "Spirit of the adoption of sons, whereby we cry: Abba, Father" (8:15), the Spirit who "asks for us with unspeakable groanings" (8:26), and whose desires in us "he that searches the hearts" knows (8:27). Through this identity of God's Spirit in God and in us is brought about the "manifestation" (parrhêsia), which is both the truth and its witness; "The Spirit gives testimony to our spirit that we are the sons of God" (8:16). On this account we have his "testimony in us" (1 Jn 5:10). But the identity in question is not to be conceived after the manner of indian philosophy, void of all content. It is one which comprises, in the Spirit

184

and in the unity of its testimony, "water and blood" (1 Jn 5:6).

Only on this plane is a real dialog possible between christianity and other religions. There cannot be dialog between a false autonomy and a true heteronomy; and this appears to be the alternative so long as we take the word of God as a bare historical fact. But it was Christ's own will to transfigure, in his death, resurrection and ascension, the whole historical character of his revelation, endowing it with a universality such that all the aspirations of human religion and mysticism are caught up into it and surpassed to an infinite degree. And the unutterable bliss of the mystical experience wherein the finite spirit is freed of all limitations and taken up into the infinite Spirit, the bliss which the sages of China, India and of sufism agree in valuing so highly, finds its fulfillment in the "marriage" through the Spirit between God and creation. Only here the liberation has nothing negative about it. It is not brought about by an ascetic denial of all that is finite as illusion and maya but by union in love with the Spirit of Christ; nor by one's own activity of detachment (abstraction), but by abandonment to the activity of the Spirit (agesthai). The first procedure can only lead to an identity that consists in nirvana, at the cost of discarding all finite reality; but the second leads to an identity resulting in fulfillment, where all that is finite is transfigured.

There has never been any other way by which the finite, estranged from God, could be both opened out to the infinite and raised above itself than the verbum caro. Yet Scheeben was right in treating under the title marriage even this first commercium, the union of the two natures in

Christ, together with all that is connected with it as preparation and consequence. However much the word in revelation may act in a positive, historical and juridical fashion it is always, and primarily, the expression of the divine and human connubium, whose final and perfect stage is necessarily wordless, intimately in fact, not the I-thou relationship but the sudden flashpoint of fusion. Scheeben, both in his *Mysteries of Christianity* and his *Dogmatic Theology* revived the great patristic and scholastic tradition, which alone can lead to a real dialog with the world's great religions and philosophies.

3

Hen is the characteristic word of that mysticism which ascends by renunciation of the finite. Pan is the attempt to bring back the finite despite this renunciation. "Hen kai pan" remains an aspiration of the heart which may well be postulated and assented to as the ultimate ideal, but one which it lacks any power to attain. What applies to mysticism applies also to philosophy. It can and must postulate that nothing of that which is is extraneous to the unity of being, and that in all that is the revelation of being is to be discerned; but it cannot prove, or desire to prove, that the creature is coincident with the creator or simply a mode of him. From the hen to the pan—the two, after all, belong together—the bridge joining them can only be thrown by God. If this bridge is what the christian religion consists in, then "there arises the infinite demand that the content of religion should vindicate itself also to thought, and this necessity is not to be eluded."

These are the words of Hegel (*Philosophy of Religion* 1832, II, 280). His theology and philosophy of the Spirit stand face to face. The positive cannot be the ultimate. "The bible has this positive form, though it is one of its proverbs that the letter kills, but the spirit gives life. So the question is which spirit applies, which spirit makes the word come alive. . . . It is the spirit which begins, in this manner, with the positive, but which is essentially present: it must be the true, the right, the holy Spirit, who comprehends and knows the divine and this content as divine" (165–66). Thus "religion is more closely determined as the self-consciousness of God" (151) and revelation, at its height the incarnation of God, as its full explication. "This history is the explication of the divine nature itself" (250). God had to become man, otherwise the hen and the pan would remain separate for eternity. But only in one single man could God become incarnate, for the asiatic mind is always prone to the view that "dwelling in the body and becoming singular and individualized is an abasement of the spirit. Therein consists the determination of the untruth, of the purely material side, of immediate existence. But, on the other hand, the determination of immediate existence is, at the same time, an essential one, the culminating expression of the spirit in its subjectivity. . . . The factor of immediate existence is contained in the spirit itself. . . . The natural is not an extrinsic necessity, but the spirit as its subject, in its infinite relationship to itself, has the determination of immediateness therein. If then the nature of the spirit and the nature of God is to be revealed to men

187

in the whole development of the idea, to that extent this form must also occur in it, and this is precisely the form of finitude" (236). Therefore Christ is "son of God and son of man; this is simply to be accepted; the true sense of this expression cannot be explained away" (248). And when he dies for all the world, then "God has died, God is dead—this is the most terrifying thought, all truth is not, negation itself is in God" (249). But the resurrection annuls this finitude, including death, and is the proof of the power of the spirit, which is absolute self-presence (276), and, as "community consciousness" of the reconcilation between God and the world, signifies the true transfiguration of the history of God in Jesus. The limits are justified in that they are transcended, and from them result the concreteness, the determination of God as totality. "The form, the determination, is not only finitude, the limit, but (as) form, as totality of form(s), is itself the concept, and these forms exist necessarily and essentially" (286). For this reason true philosophy can only be theology, for only God is "the absolute truth; and so nothing else has any value as compared with God and his explication." But for this reason this last thing is also true: "Thought is the absolute judge, before which the content has to justify and vindicate itself" (287). "Philosophy . . . sets forth the reconciliation of God with himself and with nature; it means that nature, the being-other, is in itself divine" (288).

Thus there is a communication for the hen to the pan over the bridge of the trinity and the incarnation of God, but in such wise that the finite and the infinite Spirit are identical; and God cannot find himself otherwise than in man. It is certainly a transfiguration of history, but one in

188

which prayer and the "unspeakable groaning of the Spirit" are replaced by the concept and a knowledge which is anything but groaning, and ultimately by a grotesque collapse of spirituality.

The sphere of the Spirit which arches over the historical word of God is quite a different one. The hen units itself to the pan ("to be panta en pasin"—1 Cor 15:28) in a freedom which no concept can comprise and for which no philosophy is appropriate. For this reason the kingdom of God cannot be confined within historical time, neither in the prophetic form of Joachim of Flora nor in the philosophical form of Hegel; it must always remain open, eschatologically, in the new aeon. We are only granted an "earnest," a "foretaste," a guarantee of what is to come, not a delivery; "for we are saved by hope . . . for what a man sees, why does he hope for?" (Rom 8:24). It is not the conscious concept that arches over the word, but the yearning Spirit of consolation which, as such, guarantees the freedom and all the gifts of insight.

The word of God has come forth into history from the silence and secrecy of God; this the martyr Ignatius understood correctly. And Paul before him took his stand on this historical event. "My evangelium", side by side with the "kerygma of Jesus Christ," is preached "according to the revelation of the mystery which was kept *secret* from eternity" (Rom 16:25). And to the Colossians he wrote that they may be "instructed in the charity . . . and in the knowledge of the mystery of God the father and of Christ Jesus, in whom are *hid* all the treasures of wisdom and knowledge" (Col 2:2–3); to the Ephesians that they "may understand my knowledge in the mystery of Christ, which in other generations *was not known* to the sons of men, as it is now revealed to his holy apostles and prophets in the Spirit" (Eph 3:4–5). Yet we must observe that the content of this secret, now revealed, is not solely the positive word of scripture or of Jesus in the gospel, nor taken by itself the redemption by his death, but rather what is contained, yet hidden, in the incarnation, namely the *"unsearchable* riches of Christ" and "the dispensation of the mystery which has been *hidden* from eternity in God, who created all things" (Eph 5:9–9). This means therefore that hidden and enclosed in the world plan of the creator rests the plan to reestablish, in the fullness of time, all things in heaven and earth in Christ the head (Eph 1:10), a plan that even when proclaimed cannot be understood but which demands that "you be strengthened by his Spirit with might unto the inward man; that Christ may dwell by faith in your hearts; that, being rooted and founded in charity, you may be able to comprehend, with all the saints, what is the breadth and length and height and depth, to know also the charity of Christ which surpasses all knowledge; that you may be filled unto all the fullness of God" (Eph 3:16–19).

If the word was silent previously it is now, according to revelation, so rich and luxuriant (hyperbole, perisseuein) that further speech and utterance fails, and we are reduced to a knowledge of how greatly love surpasses knowledge. This is truly going beyond thought into act, not our own act but God's act in us; it means giving up our own knowledge in order to be possessed by God's knowledge (1 Cor 8:3; 13:12; 2 Cor 5:11; Gal 5:9; Eph 2:10; Phil 3:12; Jn 6:28–29) This is Spirit. This is religion. This is both the fulfillment and the elimination of all history. But the relationship of logos and Spirit cannot be contained in any concept. If the Spirit proceeded from the logos alone then it would perhaps be the glorification of the word alone, as its highest emanation. But the Spirit also proceeds from the father, and does so inasmuch as the son looks back to the father in eternity and returns to him in time. This means that the word, which became and remains flesh, is glorified as *returning to its origin;* only as such will he come again to bring the world to an end, and home to the eternal silence of the father.